THE AUTOBIOGRAPHY OF
KINGSLEY FAIRBRIDGE

With a Preface by
THE RIGHT HON. L. S. AMERY, P.C.
and an Epilogue by
SIR ARTHUR LAWLEY, K.C.M.G.

OXFORD UNIVERSITY PRESS
LONDON : HUMPHREY MILFORD
1927

Printed in England at the OXFORD UNIVERSITY PRESS
By John Johnson Printer to the University

SOME men, they say,
Strew rags about the shrine
Whereat they pray,
Having naught else to give.
Thus, all of mine—
Each hope wherein I live
I bring at last to you.

Dear, on my knees
I bring another failure;
In your hands
I lay this gift.

PREFACE

This is a wonderful book. It is in form the simple story of a boy's adventures in the early days of Rhodesia, ending with a few brief reminiscences of his years as a Rhodes Scholar at Oxford. If it were nothing more it would rank high among autobiographies. The making of Rhodesia as seen by a boy, his experiences with natives, his encounters with danger in every shape from wild beasts and far deadlier fever, England and Oxford seen with the eyes of one who had never lived in cities or known the conventional life of our public schools— all these things are told with amazing vividness and often with an arresting beauty of unstudied style. Much is no doubt due to the care and judgement with which Miss V.F. Boyson has arranged and edited the material left in somewhat ragged form, but the essential stuff to work on was there. The story of the death of his first sable bull or of the trapping of Ingwi, the leopard who had shadowed him nightly for months, are just instances which occur to me among many for which the book would well bear comparison even with Sir Percy Fitz-Patrick's 'Jock of the Bushveld'. Nor, I think, could any future collection of the literature of boxing do without the tale of the three fights in which he won his middle-weight ' blue ' from Julian Grenfell. They have both gone since, the one leaving the memory of every manly grace and accomplishment and some lines of poetry that will live, the other having laid the foundations of something that may yet help to change the face of the British world.

For this book is much more than a mere string of adventures and impressions. It is a Pilgrim's Progress, the story of a vision seen by a famished, fainting boy of twelve in the noon-day glare of the veld—the vision of a waste land filled with homesteads—converted by the sights of London streets into a definite purpose, that of regenerating the childhood of our slums in the more spacious life of the new lands. That vision and purpose run through all the story from that first day to the great night when a roomful of undergraduates were fired by the young Rhodes Scholar's enthusiasm to sub-scribe five shillings each to start the Child Emigra-tion Society. How that venture, based on nothing but the inspired faith of its founder, became the Fairbridge Farm School in Western Australia, and how that wonderful institution grew to what it is to-day, are told in a brief epilogue by Sir Arthur Lawley.

Kingsley Fairbridge was a man whose unquestion-ing, selfless devotion to an idea lifted him entirely above the common run, one of those 'warriors of the sighting brain' whose lives are a song and star to lead their generation. To know him was an inspiration and a privilege. How great was that privilege I only fully understood when I read this simple self-revelation of his heroic soul.

L. S. AMERY.

November 17, 1926.

CONTENTS

EPILOGUE

I

EARLY DAYS

Dreamers by Usk and Avalon,
Dwellers by Uricon or Dee . . .
Seers norland-born, sail south with me ! . . .
More fiefs hath Faeryland than one !

ARTHUR SHEARLY CRIPPS.
(*Faerylands forlorn.*)

I WAS born in 1885, in a seven-roomed cottage in Grahamstown. My parents were born in South Africa, and so were my grandparents. My father's people were partly of London, and partly of Orkney descent; my mother's people were Scots and English. The Orkney side of the family can, it is said, be traced back to Robert Stewart, Earl of Orkney (the natural son of James V), whose son, cruel Patrick, built Scalloway Castle in Zetland, and for his misdeeds was beheaded in 1614 at the market cross of Edinburgh.

My father was a land surveyor to the Cape government, and not long after I was born my mother went with him on a long wagon tour, taking me with her. We were away travelling over rough roads, from farm to farm, for a year or more.

When I was about five we went north, to Gong Gong in Griqualand West. The place was called 'Gong Gong' because of the noise the stones made when the Vaal River came down. You could hear them quite plainly at the cataract—*gong, gong, gong !*

A sister was born about this time, and my father told me that a stork brought her over the Vaal. The Vaal interested me very much. Once I fell in, and should have been drowned had not my uncle seen my head bobbing about. Another time there was a flood, and drowned sheep and cattle and great pumpkins came floating by.

When I was six we went back to Grahamstown. We drove first from Gong Gong to Barkly West in the post-cart, and then we took the train. When we got to De Aar we were very sad, because there my father left us; he was going to Cape Town, to take a boat for up-country. Next day I nearly got left behind—at Alicedale Junction I think it was. My mother sent me to get her a cup of tea and some grapes. I was walking carefully back with them when the train started off. I let the tea go and made a dash for the train with the grapes. My mother leaned out of the window and caught me by the collar. She and my nurse together managed to get me in ; but the grapes suffered in the process.

In Grahamstown we stayed with a Mr. and Mrs. Wedderburn. Mr. Wedderburn was a wagon-builder six days of the week and preached in the Wesleyan chapel on Sundays. I admired him ; he used to get shavings in his beard and on his spacious black clothes, he walked majestically through the yards and shops with a smile for every one—even for the lad Jim who had epileptic fits and could not be relied on. Sometimes he would strip off his black coat and wield a mighty hammer when they beat red-hot tyres on to the hissing stinkwood felloes. You had to be very quick or the iron got cold ; then you tipped the whole wheel into a water trough, before the wood burst into flame. He used to measure the great baulks of timber; then you could see how short and thick his hands were, and how his thumbs bent back when he leaned on them, and were very broad and flat—like a carpenter's pencil.

But on Sundays he was a different man. He objected to me playing tennis against the side of the house, and confiscated the ball. He wore a long-tailed coat, and looked hot and uncomfortable, and was always in a bad temper after the midday dinner. I chose Sunday for stealing his Castle Kennedy figs, which he carefully covered with muslin to keep off the *meisvogels*.[1] Once I ate a number of unripe ones which made my lips remarkably sore, and he looked on this as a judgement. I have been told that one of my few good points at this time was my gentleness to animals. I always rescued flies that fell into the golden syrup, and used to save hundreds at a time by opening Mrs. Wedderburn's fly-catcher when she was out of the kitchen. Sometimes I spent whole mornings watching ants bringing in grass-seeds to their holes, or emigrating in long black strings across the burnt-up turf. Round about Cradock Dam and the Mountain Drive I tried to rescue toc-tockies[2] from the ant-bear holes, but I often came too late and the patient little things were dead.

At times I was sent for change of air to a Mrs. Lanham at a farm called Stoneham. It was a wonderful place—wild and rocky and surrounded by great hills. Old Mr. Lanham was a particular friend of mine; I used to help him count his sheep as they were turned out of the

[1] Muis vogel (*Cape Dutch* ' *muisfo'el* '), or *mouse bird*.
[2] Toktokje (*Cape Dutch*), *a beetle which makes a curious tapping noise, apparently with its abdomen.*

kraals at sunrise; and in the lambing season he and
I used to wander among the bents and boulders of the
wind-swept hills to find and carry back the little lambs.
When he clipped the ostriches I held the feathers for
him. Whenever he went round the farm a horse was
saddled up for me, and I went with him.

He was a little wizened man with twinkling eyes, and he
told me all about farms, and how people lost their fingers
by putting their hands, instead of a mealie-cob, into the
husking machine. He showed me where the wild-dogs
had driven a flock of ostriches over a krantz, and where,
in the early days, he had shot a Hottentot who had stolen
and was skinning one of his sheep. When I saw the place
it looked quite ordinary—just a bare rock and a clump
of assegai-boom [1] behind a stone wall, where a yellow
cock-a-vic [2] called to his mate. He taught me how to
follow the little grey and white honey-birds that take you
to wild bees' nests, and showed me the spoor of jackal,
porcupine, and rhebok, and where the paddervanger [3] had
built her home by the stream. He used a long Snider
rifle which was too heavy for me unless I rested the
barrel in a tree-fork. But he did not shoot often, he preferred seeing the animals alive; only to jackals and wild
cats he was implacable, and those he shot or poisoned he
hung up in a big tree by the roadside, by way of a warning
to others.

The farm-house was built of stone, and on the walls
hung knob-kerries, assegais, battle-axes, and the bows

---

[1] Asgaai-boom (*Cape Dutch*), *the assegai tree.*

[2] Kook-a-vic, *the green-plumaged Bush shrike.*

[3] Paddavanger (*Dutch*), *toad-catcher, also known as the hammer-
kop, a bird of a dull brown colour, which builds an immense nest.*

and poisoned arrows of Bushmen. Mrs. Lanham and her daughter Jane had also hung up nests of the long-necked finch and bunches of everlastings. The kitchen was a cool and beautiful place where one could always get a long drink of sour calabash-milk during the day, and at dawn steaming coffee and rusks before going out to the lands. Swallows built under the eaves amongst the grape-vine, which had been grown from a raisin seed.

My father was pioneering in Mashonaland. Once many weeks passed without a letter from him. First the post-office people said the Mashonaland mails had been delayed by the rains; then they said the mails were lost in the floods. My mother never went out except to the post-office. At last, after four months, a great pile of letters came. They were written on all kinds of paper—brown and white, and some on the backs of condensed milk labels. Some of them were in envelopes bearing the beautiful eightpenny stamp of the Chartered Company, and some were in cloth wrappers, sewn with coloured thread. My mother opened them all and spread them about her bedroom table; at first she read none of them, but cried very much and would not be comforted. I watched her, wondering, and after a while I fell asleep.

Dad's letters to me were illustrated with little pictures and contained all manner of interesting things : a scrap of tough leather from an elephant's ear, hairs from a buffalo's tail, little flakes of Mashonaland gold; and he told me fine tales of the veld. One was about three men who were trekking to Fort Salisbury with a wagon. They were going through thick bush—lion country. Two of them lay in the tent at the after-end of the wagon, and the third walked behind chatting with them. It was broad noon, and very hot, and presently the two men fell asleep. When they woke again the third man was gone. They sat up and called to the drivers; but the drivers had not seen him. So they stopped the wagon, and went back shouting and calling for their friend. They hunted in the bush and fired shots, and tried to pick up the spoor. But they heard nothing, and could find nothing, and they never saw him again.

After a time we left Grahamstown and went to Cape Town. We stayed for a while with my grandmother, Mrs. Seymour Fairbridge, at ' Highstead ', Rondebosch. The Highstead grounds adjoined the famous Groote Schuur property, they ran up the flank of the Devil's Peak, and were mostly covered with pines. I built my-self a little hut near the stream where the arums grew, which divided Groote Schuur from Highstead. You could get quite inside the hut if you took your hat off. We stayed mostly, however, at Muizenberg, a little village by the sea, where I made several friends. With them I went swimming and fishing; we built rafts and collected shells and mossje's[1] eggs. But I enjoyed most my solitary rambles up the hill-side among the ghokums[2] and strange flowers, or on the white dunes beyond the Sand River where the wind-blown sea-sand cut one's bare legs like thousands of little knives—I was happy in any bare place beneath the sky, where I could hear the sea, or the wind blowing through the grass.

When I was eight years old we returned to Grahams-town and Mrs. Wedderburn, and my schooling began in earnest. I was sent to St. Andrew's preparatory school. At first I was miserable, and indeed school never interested

---

[1] *Cape sparrow.*   [2] *Hottentot ' gaukum ', or Hottentot fig.*

me; but I rose steadily, and in time reached the first form in St. Andrew's College. History and geography I liked, and would cheerfully have given all my time to these two subjects. As things were, the greater part of my day was spent in obstructing my taskmasters and drawing sketches of their faces.

My father was then coming backwards and forwards to us from Rhodesia. He was in Grahamstown in 1896, and had an office in the High Street to which I went with him every morning to help him with his survey calculations. He had an idea that I should become a surveyor and was putting me through the first steps. We used to pass the post office, and here one morning we saw a telegram pinned up, with the news of Doornkop and the capture of Dr. Jameson.[1] Dad stood close up to the telegram and said nothing. He waited like this for so long that at last I looked up at him, and tears were running down his sunburnt cheeks.

When I was eleven Dad wrote and told us to come to Rhodesia, and I was very glad. People at Grahamstown thought it was a wild and barbarous country, unfit for any civilized being. A crowd of people came to the station to see us off. The train steamed out and I was relieved to see the last of them.

[1] *He left Pitsani Potlogo, in the Bechuanaland Protectorate, for the disastrous march on Johannesburg, 29 December, 1898.*

II

A NEW WORLD

Behold, my son, the wheel-scarr'd road!
  Be shamed, and be afraid,
For we, the first, were greater men
  Than those for whom we made.
We wrought in death and hunger,
  We fought the veld—we few!
Behold this effort of our hands,
  This road we built for you.

Veld Verse.

FROM Port Elizabeth we swept out to the Indian Ocean
and I turned my back on the old world. At Durban we
were waited on at the Royal Hotel by urbane Indians,
and the Zulu ricksha boys interested me.

At Delagoa Bay we were boarded by Portuguese
officials. They were undersized, snappish little people,
composed mostly of uniforms and accoutrements. And
so we came to Beira, and my father came out to meet
us. He was, for a South African, a small man, dark,
very active and eager looking; his beard was black, and
his wavy dark hair stood up from his forehead. He wore
a bright red cummerbund, and he carried his flannel
jacket over one of his bare brown arms. He stood up in
the stern of the boat, and looked very fine as he bent to
the beat of the oars.

We took tickets to the railhead by the famous Beira
railway. This was one of England's gifts to the world.
Scores of Englishmen and hundreds of coolies and

Kafirs had died in the building of it. It ran through a hundred miles of low-veld, where dysentery, malaria, and wild beasts had swept off the contractors and their men as the August fires sweep off the long grass. Parts of it lay through steaming forests, and parts through mighty swamps where the track sank under water in the February rains. We saw great herds of game, and men fired at them from the open trucks—we travelled first, so we had a tarpaulin over our truck, and deck chairs. A herd of zebras raced the train for a long while, and we all shouted at them. Our train did not run off the rails, but most trains did, and then the passengers had to get out and push them back again. One night I heard a man say that if Mr. Kipling had known the Beira railway he would have written the finest story in the world. We left the train at the railway head, Chimoio, and went on by wagon. At Revue Bridge we saw one of the bridge-builders making a little cross for a friend who had just died of blackwater; before the last of the wagons left the outspan he too was dead.

Near Massikessi we came on the first signs of rinderpest. In a big outspan on the left-hand side of the road stood six or eight wagons. The chains and yokes were all tumbled about, and the wagons were quite deserted. Their loads were gone, and there was no sign of the owners except the cold ash of the camp fires. The cattle lay everywhere, some amongst the wagons and some in the middle of the road; down at the drift they were very thick, and many lay half in the pools where they had fallen and died. The rinderpest had come sweeping down from the north, and my father, who had been out shooting on the Pungwe Flats, said that the buffalo were dying in vast numbers. During the afternoon we caught up some wagons driving composite spans; in one span I noticed bulls, cows, oxen, donkeys, a mule, and a horse.

From Massikessi Dad, mother, and my sister Hilda went on by coach; I remained with the wagons. We had come to the great mountains of the high-veld; to left and to right they towered, and ahead lay the long high ridge which runs roughly from Bulawayo to Manica-land and is called 'The Divide'. The wagons wound in and out along the Revue Valley, and we rose by degrees from the land of palms and bamboos to the cooler plateau of Murawha's country. So we came upon the flat space between two mountain streams, where the town of Umtali now stands. In those days it was all bush and long grass. Findley's trading-store stood near one of the streams; half a mile away were Russell's two huts, and on the flank of the vast Inyamutshura Range were Fisher's huts. But beyond this it was all wilderness. South of the road rose a low stony ridge, beyond the ridge a great range called the Dora Mountains; far westward jutted Imyarugwi—the Place of Leopards—and all the bare rock-peaks of the Odzi country. After-wards I got to know them all. I learnt to hunt among the valleys, and to view new country from the wind-swept summits. They taught me thirst and hunger, exhaustion and endeavour. I found masses of orchids on the summit of Dora, and strange short grasses along the brow of Vumba, where the shy blue-buck darted in the ravines and the wind thundered all night above the precipice.

Late in the afternoon we breasted Christmas Pass, creeping up between the rocks of Murawha's Kopje and the wooded flanks of Inyamutshura. At dawn we came to Umtali, and the wagons outspanned. I left the wagons to look for my father's house. The Central Hotel had a double layer of sandbags piled along the verandah; for the Mashona were in rebellion, and fighting was going on in Makoni's country to the north-west. Every one seemed asleep, but I knocked at Corderoy and Reynolds's store, and Mr. Reynolds said that Dad was in hospital and that my mother was staying with the nurses, but they expected to be back at home that same day. He pointed out ' Fairbridge's Kopje ', and gave me the key of the house. I walked out in the light of sunrise, passing the sentries at the Camp, and came to the kopje—a small hill covered with thorns and umsasa and umhondo, which in those days were strange trees to me. And on the other side of the kopje, near its summit, was my father's house.

There were two buildings, the house and the kitchen. Both had mud walls, but the house was thatched, whilst the kitchen had a galvanized iron roof. The windows were made of calico, tacked across a frame. I used my key on the padlock and went in; there were two rooms, both very small, divided by a six-foot high partition. A low bed stood in one room, and a hammock was slung in the other. On a table made of rough poles and packing cases lay a quantity of tin plates, some black-handled knives and forks, two or three enamelled mugs of different sizes, and a number of jam and kipper tins with their edges carefully knocked down. The jam tins, I discovered later, made excellent cups ; while the kipper tins, being long and shallow, could be used either as vegetable dishes or as porridge plates.

Mother, I think, found life difficult. There were no comforts whatever. Nearly everything we ate came out of tins—*petits pois*, *champignons*, condensed milk, Danish butter (in hot weather this was a yellow oil in which white curds floated), army rations, bully beef, plum-pudding, Canterbury cake, and so on. On Christmas Eve our beautifully labelled plum-pudding turned out to be the evil-smelling mixture of boiled mutton and carrots known as 'army rations'. Mother used to make our bread, and it was kept in a large biscuit tin; I remember that two of our goats got at it once and walked about the yard with their heads stuck in the tin, like Siamese twins. Goat was not very good eating, but we sometimes had it—for a treat. Mashona fowls too were expensive, but we had them and got deadly sick of them; I have heard men say they couldn't look a fowl in the face. Our fowls were supposed to lay, but unless they chose the bed or hammock for this operation (and when once they had fixed upon the hammock it was hard to change their purpose) they laid their eggs away out among the long grass and red-plum bushes, and one knew nothing of them till one day a hen would come clucking to the house with five or six nimble little chicks. The kites and hawks used to swoop down under our very noses, and—away went hen, chickens, or even roosters! One night a leopard killed my favourite goat right under our verandah, but my father chased the brute and fired at it; and we ate the goat.

I strongly objected to the discomfort, and said so. I kept on saying so, until one day my father took me aside.

'Look here, Sonny,' he said, 'you don't seem very contented.'

'No,' I answered, 'I think this is a pretty beastly place.'

'Well,' said my father, 'the fact is you haven't got enough to do. Now, I'll give you the choice of two things: you can either go back to St. Andrew's College or you can stay at Umtali. But if you stay at Umtali *you must work*! Think it over and let me know.'

I decided, in about a second, to work.

'Perhaps you would like a hut of your own,' said my father, 'and if so, you must build it.'

My father suggested that I should raise an old wagon that stood at the foot of the kopje on to a low stone wall, build stones up around the wheels, and pitch a tent on top. The underneath compartment could be used as an office, and the upper part with its tent for a bedroom. He volunteered to help me.

We borrowed some screw-jacks, and hoisted up the wagon. We built a stone wall under the wheels, and, with the help of some of my father's boys, other rudimentary walls between the wheels and at the back. We hung a piece of calico in front, weighted with pebbles, for a door. On the wagon itself we pitched a small fly-tent; my happiness, when I slept in it for the first time, was complete. I was no less happy when early one morning, while I was still abed, some transport rider fired a shot down the Salisbury road, and the bullet ripped through the canvas.

Then my father gave me his survey calculations to work out. I had already done some of this sort of thing in Grahamstown, so it was not strange to me; in fact I became so proficient at it that my father was obliged to lower the price—he paid me by piece work. And in this manner, at the age of eleven, I began to earn my own living.

One day, about this time, a great weariness came upon me. My body ached all over, and my eyes hurt so that I could not do the calculations. I wandered out from our wagon-office in search of something to drink, for I was very thirsty. No matter how much I drank I always wanted more. My head buzzed and I could not hear or see properly. Finally I went round to the back of the house, and was very sick.

Then I was undressed and put to bed. I dreamed of great thunder-storms and pelting rain, and then that my father and I were sleeping together coiled up round a turnstile in Grahamstown. It was early morning, and people on both sides wanted to come through the turnstile. I tried to wake my father, to let them pass, but I could not. I shook him and shook him. . . .

This was my first knowledge of the great Grey Thief, malaria. Wander as I will, turn or double in my tracks as I may, he has gone ever with me. When I have nothing to do, he, too, does nothing. But in the times of stress and endeavour he winds his mighty arms about me and tries to drag me down. So that all my life I have had, as it were, to fight each battle twice.

III

CECIL RHODES

Dreamer devout, by vision led
Beyond our guess or reach,
The travail of his spirit bred
Cities in place of speech.
So huge the all-mastering thought that drove—
So brief the term allowed—
Nations, not words, he linked to prove
His faith before the crowd.

RUDYARD KIPLING.

DAD had some surveying to do among the mountains round Shitaka's kraal, and mother went to stay with Mrs. Fisher beyond Christmas Pass. I had another touch of fever and was spending a week in hospital. When I was better Mrs. Sandy Tulloch gave me a tiny terrier pup, which I called 'Viking', and I got a lift on a wagon to the Fishers' huts.

Upon Viking I rapidly concentrated an immense amount of affection, but to my grief he rolled off my bed one day snapping at flies, and never moved again. I took his poor, limp, little corpse, and buried it under a wild custard-apple. I had dreamed that he and I would have great adventures together when we grew older, and it was terrible when he lay so quietly in my hands. I made a little wooden cross and wrote his name on it, and had the last real cry of my childhood beside his grave.

I went back to the huts and said I was going to find my father. They tried to dissuade me—especially as it was but a few days since I left the hospital—but I was determined. Early next morning I started out quite alone, and walked the ten miles to Old Umtali. Here I made inquiries, and was directed to Maritz's huts, six miles away on the Gold Belt. I had been there before with my father, so I started out at once. In the early afternoon I arrived, and told Mr. Maritz that I was looking for Dad, and that I came from Fisher's huts. He looked curiously at me, and said that Dad was some miles farther on, up the Imbeza River. I was for going on at once, but Mr. Maritz told me to wait awhile ; two of his boys were going to Shitaka's kraal and they would point out my father's tent.

I found my father next day camped on the Divide. This was a country of mists and rounded hills. Flat-topped thorns grew on the flanks, and wild bananas in the valleys. Each valley had its mountain stream, often falling in pretty cascades, and there was one near Shitaka's kraal lined with maidenhair fern and shaded by lemon trees.

We worked for some weeks along the Gold Belt, till I got to learn the many tiny paths that dodged and hid and scrambled up hill and down dale, making progress possible among the sarsaparilla and foot-hill scrub. Camping and re-camping we returned slowly to Maritz's place at Umtali-Imbeza. There we heard that Mr. Cecil Rhodes was expected to visit the Gold Belt of Penha-longa.

One blazing day, when the sun swam in cloudless blue and the brown larks were soaring and clapping their

wings, my father, who was using the theodolite, suddenly turned towards me—

'Sonny,' he said, 'there is Mr. Rhodes.'

I looked down the hillside, and on the Penhalonga
road at the foot of the hill, crossing the Imbeza drift,
came a Cape cart and six mules. The mules halted at
the foot of the Umtali road, and three men alighted and
began slowly to climb the ascent towards the huts on the
Sabi Ophir mine.

My father packed up the theodolite and went down
the hill.

Just in front of the huts stood an immense fig-tree, of
a kind uncommon in those parts. On the verandah of the
main hut sat Mr. Rhodes, bare-headed, with his hands
clasped on his lap. He looked straight out into the sunshine, down the valley of the Umtali River. Across the
valley on the left stood Maritz's huts, and here and there
along the ridge you could see the tin claim-plates of
reef properties. On the right stood Fort Hill, crowned
with its walls of earth and stone—the citadel of the men
of the early days.

I knew that great trouble had befallen Mr. Rhodes.
My father had told me that his best friend, Dr. Jameson,
had been put in jail; that Mr. Rhodes himself had
resigned, or was about to resign, his public appointments
both in England and South Africa.

I knew these things because every one knew them. To
Rhodesians Cecil Rhodes was something more than human,
he was Rhodes, the Colossus; and now he was brought
low. After the trouble caused by the Jameson 'raid'
came the rinderpest, which swept down over Southern
Rhodesia wrecking the fortunes of pioneers. Then the

rebellion of the Matabele was followed by the unexpected uprising of the Mashona [1]—rescued by him from the ferocious Matabele—and these together caused the death of many men who loved him. Moreover the rebellions had laid heavy financial burdens on the Chartered Company. The ' raid ' had left dissensions, and many of Rhodes's old associates at the Cape had turned their backs on him. Finally Groote Schuur, his beautiful house near my old playground on the Devil's Peak, had been burnt to the ground, and with it the treasures of old Dutch and Huguenot art which he had spent years in collecting. All had happened in that one year of 1896, and men said he was greatly changed and that his hair had turned white.

But that day at the Sabi Ophir Mr. Rhodes seemed strong and quiet, as he looked out over the land— ' great spaces washed with sun '—that he had won for the Empire.

My father took off his hat and walked up to him, and they shook hands. Then Mr. Rhodes shook hands with me, and smiled in a deep and far-off way. I was silent, listening to all that was said. We lunched together, and they talked until late in the afternoon, and it seems strange now that I can remember no word of what was said.

If I might go back again to that one day ! If only I had had then even the little wit that I have now ! I should have said ' Take me, take me, and let me serve you ! '

Before six years had passed he was dead.

[1] *The term Mashona is not used by the natives, but is a generic term distinguishing the allied tribes of the eastern divisions of Southern Rhodesia from the Matabele in the west.*

Fourteen years later I was at Oxford. Round me were young men from Australia and from New Zealand, from Canada and from South Africa, from the West Indies and from Newfoundland, from the United States and from Germany. Of all those hundred and sixty men brought by Rhodes from afar to be that night together, I alone, I think, had seen and spoken to him.

IV

UMTALI

The dust lay thick on the burning road,
And thick on thorn and umsasa too;
All thick it lay where the bare rock showed,
And the rough roadside where the long grass grew.

Less than a mile away my eyes
In the wilder early days had seen
The charred sticks on the sloping rise
Where the Shangaan impi's camp had been.

Veld Verse.

KIND Mrs. Tulloch had made good the loss of Viking by giving me another pup of the same litter, which we called ' Vixen '. Vic as a puppy accompanied us round the Gold Belt hills, and early in 1897 went over Christmas Pass with Dad and me to the survey of various residential sections in New Umtali. Umtali was a township thrice located. It began at the Umtali River, near Penhalonga; it was moved from thence six miles to the plain beyond the Inyomgombie River. Then with the approach of the Beira railway it was decided once more to shift it, this time ten miles southwards, to where it now stands; the steep gradients of the Divide making it practically impossible for the railway to mount the high-veld in any other place.

This was a fine and busy time. Every one had received ' compensation ' from the Chartered Company, and was beginning to rebuild in New Umtali. They prophesied that with the advent of the railway would come cheaper food, more capital, and a general boom. All day long wagons and carriers toiled over Christmas Pass, raising great clouds of red dust. Strings of ' boys' camped by the little streams near Christmas Pass Hotel, and the charred fuel of the last impi of Gungunyana went to boil their *sadza*.[1] The wood and iron houses of Old Umtali were taken down and carried over the Pass. Building on a grand new scale was started on the plains of Murawha —some of it never to be completed. The words ' transport' and ' contracts ' were in every one's mouth. Dad, Vic, and I went over the Pass in a Cape cart with six mules.

Great gangs of boys from Nyungwe [2] and Senna were working on the streets that were to be. Mabandawi and Magorongoza dug side by side, trenching the two streams that flanked the township; the deadly mud, packed with the germs of malaria, was cast up beside the trenches. At that time every one was too busy to be ill, but they died later. This draining was sound work, however, and the two trenches have since done much to make Umtali healthy; that those who made them died when the harness of endeavour fell from their shoulders is only in keeping with the story of all pioneers. *Sic vos non vobis.*

I used to drag Dad's survey chain. Vic and I were always together, and very much in touch with Mother Earth. I pulled the fore end of the chain, Dad aligned me, and I knelt to put in the survey-pin; so the white sand at the Paulington and Darlington ends of the township,

---

[1] *The staple food of thick reddish porridge, made from millet meal. Cf. Bishop Knight-Bruce's translation of the Lord's Prayer: ' Utipe nasi sadza redu remisiyesi ' (Give us this day our daily bread).*

[2] *Or Tete.*

and the red clay and blue diorite boulders of the Utopia
end, became very familiar to me. Masitembo of Senna,
our boss-boy and a great teller of folk-lore, used to conduct the tree-felling and grass-cutting operations. He
was always neat and spotless in his white singlet and
calico loin-cloth; a little man, beautifully made, he
carried his chin in the air and his chest thrown out.
When I sat sweating and exhausted in the dust, Masitembo stood out in the flood of sunlight, all keenness
and energy. ‘ *Apalemwe*,’ he shouted, ‘ *bwena kuno* !’
‘Little friends, food is ready...’ And the shaggy Mabudja,[1]
with their hair tied up in bark and strung with red beads,
obeyed.

The site of New Umtali was filled with life and
energy. The commonage rang with the sound of axes.
Everywhere the builders were sinking the foundations of
stores and houses; over at Darlington every noon and
morning the veld thundered to the quarry dynamiters.
Beyond Blackwater Spruit the brickmakers were busy.
So we, too, when the survey work was finished, built
three pondokie[2] huts of poles and grass on the Utopia
property; and my father made arrangements with a
mason to build a stone house near by.

Those were spacious times. Men spoke always of
progress and development; a new era was beginning,
and the grind and death and danger of the Early Days
was over. So my father called his property ‘ Utopia ’.
The keen burnt faces of the men of those days are even

---

[1] *Mabudja or Mabushla, a warlike tribe living in the neighbour-
hood of the Mazoe.*

[2] Pondok (*Cape Dutch*), *a hut, from Malay* pond'ok, *a stage-house
or leaf shelter. The colonial term is applied to a primitive kind of hut.*

now in my eyes; and I remember, too, that we carried
many of them across the Commonage Spruit to the fenced
acre beyond the Camp. Some of them went in Wilkie's
donkey cart with its two black donkeys, unattended;
and others went in the gun-carriage, covered by the
Union Jack, and we marched behind with our Martinis
reversed.

My father engaged a couple of wagons, and we shifted
house from Old to New Umtali. We occupied the three
pondokies, which were quite comfortable, for the grass
still smelt fresh and warm. The contractor got to work
on the foundations of our house, and his boys collected
building stone from the round walls of the ancients[1] that
stood at the foot of the kopje. This house, like the one
we had just abandoned, was to stand on the highest
point in the town—a little rounded kopje of diorite
boulders and red clay, crowned with three fig-trees,
some kaitchipering[2] bushes, some marula trees, and
a group of queer thorn-bushes that have a very delicate
and lovely blossom. The kaitchipering have whitish-
green bark, a hardy stunted growth, and large white
flowers of a powerful and delicious odour. Wild custard-
apples grew on the east slope, and in their season
bloomed purple and yellow-and-white orchids, gladioli,
laburnums, and scarlet-shrubs. I collected many flame-
lily bulbs, and other flowers, and planted them on the
kopje; but they were wild things, and seldom took root.

[1] *The numerous ruins of stone buildings, or zimbabwe, of Rhodesia were formerly supposed to have been built in very ancient days.
They are now said to be the work of a Bantu people, and to date from
medieval days. The workmanship is primitive, and the stone used is
the local granite or diorite.*

[2] Katjepiring, *Cape Dutch for* Gardenia Thunbergia.

V

A VISION

I looked, and beheld . . .
The brown of the veld, the unending immensity,
League after league of the houseless and homeless,
The smokeless, the gardenless wealth of the desert,
The rivers unfish'd and the valleys unhunted,
An empire peopled with nothing—a country
Abandoned to emptiness, yearning for people,
A mother well fit for the birth of a nation.

Veld Verse.

UNDER the urge of a chance adventure, and driven by
pride and hunger, I found a task and dreamed a dream
which held me all the days of my boyhood, and now
occupies my every working hour, and will never be ful-
filled even though I live the eighty and odd years that
have been foretold to me.

When I was twelve years old my father offered me ten
pounds to build two small pondokies for him on his Gold
Belt property. The place was called Hygeia and lay on
a spur of the Inyamutshura Range, near Shitaka's kraal,
about eight miles from Umtali. The path lay over the
range, and was a stiff climb and a rapid descent.

I accepted the offer, and took Vixen and my boy Jack
with me. Jack was a wiry little Senna, about middle-age;
he carried my two blankets and his own, also a skoff-box [1]

[1] *From Dutch* schofttijd, *meal-time. It is now used as a general
term for food.*

with about a week's provisions. I carried a couple of axes and sickles.

We slept the first night at Shitaka's kraal. I had seen my father give ' presents ' to native chiefs when on the veld, so I sent for Shitaka and made him a present of a couple of tins of bully beef. A long and varied experience of Kafirs has since shown me that this is a mistaken practice ; very few Kafirs like, fear, or respect a man who gives them presents. Kafirs only give when they are afraid, and wish to propitiate ; consequently they impute the same motives to white men.

I had not the slightest fear of Shitaka, but I had seen him several times before and thought it was polite to recognize him in some way. I did not realize that my father, anxious to show the raw human material of Rhodesia that the white men were friendly towards them, had quite overlooked the native attitude of mind. I gave Shitaka the tins of beef, which he took with alacrity. There was, however, a lack of grace in his thanks which immediately struck me ; he left at once, made no further acknowledgment, and never took the trouble to visit me again.

Altogether our reception was not hospitable, so next morning Jack and I moved out of the kraal and camped at Hygeia—less than a mile farther on. We at once cleared a patch of grass for the huts, and set about collecting poles. This was not difficult. Then we took the sickles and cut big bundles of grass, because thatching-grass was to be found only at a considerable distance ; the lengthy journeys took time, and even then we under-estimated the amount of grass we required. The next operation was to dig the holes for the two forked uprights that supported the roof-tree. We had then to erect the framework and put on the thatch.

In seven days everything was complete except the thatch, this part we had not yet begun. But food was giving out. I spoke to Jack about it, and gave him five shillings to buy some pumpkins and ufu[1] at the kraal. Several days previously a party of young native girls and men had come to trade; they were very noisy, and evidently wished to impress us with the fact that *they*, at any rate, hadn't much respect for white men. When I attempted to trade with them the girls all clapped their hands and went into ecstasies of laughter. The young men smiled patronizingly and strutted about, looking inquisitively at our little camp. Finally, when they had played out their joke they all swung off, shouting and laughing, without selling anything.

It was, of course, simply a put-up job, the type of humour that tickles the Kafir heart. Kafirs are fond of playing it on raw Englishmen who do not understand their little ways. I, a small boy with neither rifle nor a retinue of servants, was just the person to afford them an hour's amusement. Both Jack and I kept our tempers and behaved with as much dignity as we could, but our non-chalance was hardly a fit weapon against ridicule. The only point we really scored in was in the matter of dogs. Vic detested Kafir dogs as vehemently as she did their masters, and no sooner did the slinking yellow-and-white brutes appear in the clearing than she was at them. She attacked them so tempestuously that they did not wait to be bitten, but fled with anticipatory howls into the undergrowth.

[1] *Maize meal.*

After this experience we knew that we could not expect friendly treatment, and for my part I made several resolutions about giving presents; but we did not anticipate what really happened. Jack took the five shillings and went down to Shitaka's kraal; he returned late in the evening with the five shillings and nothing more.

The Maswina,[1] he said, told him that they had nothing to sell. After a long delay, however, they told an old woman to bring some small pumpkins. She did—the smallest procurable. For each of these they demanded two shillings.

'I would not buy them, Senhor; all three were not worth sixpence. They know we have no food, and they are laughing. *Wa, zhi.*—the dogs!'

That night we ate a tin of Strasburg meat, minced up stuff meant for spreading on bread and butter. We had nothing on which to spread it so we ate it plain—Jack, Vic, and I. Next day we had water for breakfast, water for lunch, and water for dinner. Moreover we slept in water, for it rained on the night of our last meal, and the two following nights. It rained all through the day —the light, constant, soaking rain that is characteristic of the Border hills. The sun did not come out and thatching was laborious, for the grass was heavy with rain.

We had not cut enough grass, it was not even enough for one pondokie, and we used it all up by evening. The keen east wind swept over the watershed and made us bitterly cold. With great difficulty we got a fire to burn, and crouched over it in our wet things. We had been sleeping in the open, and had kept our blankets only partly dry by covering them with grass. But the grass

---

[1] Amaswina, *dogs, a term of contempt bestowed by the Matabele on the tribes of Mashonaland.*

was all used up for thatching the lower lathes, so our blankets soon got wet through.

The following day, the second of our fast, we spent cutting grass and carrying it back to the pondokies. We worked without a rest from dawn to dark. It never stopped raining; even my felt hat and my hair got wet through. My hands became very white and raw and corrugated through constantly handling the wet grass and sickle; Jack's hands became pink. Grass seeds got into my shirt and trousers, and they irritated horribly; but I could not get them out because my hands were too cramped with cold. Vixen sat about and shivered in great spasms —beginning in the middle of her body and spreading outwards to the tip of her nose and the very end of her stumpy tail. She cocked her head on one side, puckered her brows and lips, and looked inquiringly at us. Jack and I talked very little, but there was no need for us to encourage each other; we both were absolutely determined to do our work and show no sign. We had between us a sort of tacit understanding that we would not give in before the cowardly tribesmen of Shitaka's kraal.

That night the fire was more difficult than ever to light; all the wood seemed to be soaked through and through, and it was fortunate that we had kept our matches dry by covering them with an empty tin. Vic slept in my wet blankets with me, and was delightfully warm, but old Jack in his cheap, striped blanket looked very cold. I asked him if he would like to sleep with me, and keep warmer that way; but he said he was *lungilé*.[1] He never uttered a word of complaint, nor seemed

[1] *Good, right.*

to think that there was any way out of our difficulties except by showing the Maswina that he and the baas were quite independent of them and their pumpkins.

The third day ended our fast. I did not feel so hungry as the previous day, but I was rather weak and very much disinclined to help with the thatching. I am afraid Jack did more than his share. We completed the two pondokies, collected the rubbish, and threw it under the undergrowth. At about three o'clock we rolled up our blankets and started back for Umtali.

As luck would have it the sun came out, and we soon dried; but the blankets remained sodden, and must have been a heavy burden. I felt dreamy and far-away; my body seemed light, but I breathed heavily as we breasted the great slopes. Suddenly the thought came to me, ' Why are there no farms ? Why are there no people?' It came to me again and again, ' Why are there no farms *here* ?' I remembered having heard my mother say that her father had been concerned in settling the emigrants who came from England to the Cape. ' Why are there no emigrants here?' I thought. I found myself picking out little plateaux on the grassy slopes, and thinking ' There is room there for a farm.' Sometimes I spoke aloud and Jack thought I was speaking to him.

Climbing the steep and slippery hills was most exhausting. To make matters worse Vic began to shy at various objects on the footpath; first at small aloes, then at curious-looking bushes. She got so nervous that I had to go back very often and carry her past the place. She would trot quietly on ahead, and then coming face to face with an aloe, would scamper back with her hair on end. It was tiring going back for her, and stooping to pick her up made me ache. I would look into the deep valleys, where the grass was six feet high, and wish that I could see a farm. I imagined smoke coming out of the chimney, and the grass all cropped down by cattle. So the vision came to me, when I was starved and miserable: I spoke it out aloud: ' Some day I will bring farmers here.' Jack stopped and looked at me, ' Baas ? ' he said. ' Let us go on,' I said, ' it is nothing.'

When we reached the top of the range and started down the south slopes, Vic began shying at stones; so I took her in my arms and carried her the rest of the way. She was not really heavy, but she seemed so, and the steep descent shook me considerably; I was trembling all over when we got down to the flat.

At about half-past five we arrived at Utopia, and I told Jack to go and get some food from the cook. A number of people were having tea with my mother; they were all sitting in the temporary two-sided hut that we used as a living-room. They seemed to me, coming out of the profound silence of the hills, to be making a great deal of noise.

They all chaffed me for coming in to tea so unbrushed and in such dirty clothes. But I just said, ' How do you do ? ' to them and began eating hot scones. Our cook made a very good kind by mixing milk with the flour, and used to serve them hot and buttered. I ate a great many, and the people began to go away. More and more of them went away, but I kept on eating. I do not think the hot things agreed with me very well, for after a time I became unconscious.

After a few days I got better, and went out to see how Jack was getting on. Vic, I knew, was all right; they had allowed her to sleep on my bed, and ever after this whenever we were together she always slept at the foot of my blankets; but she had developed a curious little habit of whining when she was very cold, and putting her head down and rubbing her mouth with her paws.

Jack showed no ill-effects for about a fortnight. Then he began to cough, and complained of a sore throat and a 'nyoka'[1] in his inside. He got worse and worse, and finally knocked off work. We took every care of him, and gave him warm blankets and 'Balsam of Camphor' or 'Oil of Balsam'—I forget the exact name—on lumps of sugar. But he was very ill for a month or more, and at last said he wanted to go home to Senna with some friends. We gave him an axe, a bag of food, and some new blankets, and sent him off; but he was back within a week. His 'friends', he said had left him one night, taking all his money and the things we had given him. They evidently thought he was going to die, and, according to the native habit, took good care not to be present at the end; and made the best of a bad job by first rifling his person. However, this adventure had a stimulating effect on Jack's health, for in another week or two he was well.

I did not tell my people anything about our Starvation Camp for a long while afterwards, and I did not think they knew the details. But I must have let out the story while I was delirious, for, when I mentioned it, my mother said she knew all about it.

Dad, she said, had been absent for a day—having an interview with Shitaka.

---

[1] i-Nyoka, *Kafir generic term for snakes.*

VI

THE MYSTERY OF MYSINYANGA

Now, Muse, let's sing of rats.

JAMES GRAINGER.
(*The Sugar Cane.*)

Not long after my fateful expedition to Hygeia, my family all went up there and stayed at the huts I had built. We supplemented the huts with others of a more substantial sort and made the place quite comfortable.

The Leckie Ewings stayed with us, and contributed largely to my education. Mr. Leckie Ewing wrote poetry, philosophized, and composed oratorios which he sang generously to the hill winds. Mrs. Leckie Ewing, who was from Donegal, was of a more practical nature, deep-voiced, and a delightful comrade. She was already white-haired, but the strongest woman I ever knew. When I came in from a morning's wanderings amongst the hills, she used forcibly to take me to a basin of water and make me wash my grimy hands and face—not forgetting the neck—an operation which I loathed.

After a month or so of prospecting on the Gold Belt, Mr. Leckie Ewing decided to go north to Inyanga— that great range of mountains called the Mountains of the Moon. He owned a farm up there, upon which he hoped to settle. I was to go with him, taking three boys, as far as Mysinyanga, in order to build an ‘ occupation ’ hut on a property belonging to my father.

We made the journey on foot. On our first trek we crossed the famous Slippery Drift through the Chodzana, or Odzani, River, and came to the mighty pass near Umtasa's kraal.[1] Mountain and peak were almost destitute of soil; great faces of grey granite, covered with coloured lichens, loomed up on all sides; but between the barren stone of the sheer krantzes, in the vast crevices of the riven hills, and among the far-flung boulders—big as houses—that lay in the *poort*,[2] grew great numbers of Rhodesian planes, majanji, and other trees. From the steep cliffs on the left came the wild ' Bor-koom ', ' Bor-koom ' of baboons going to their caves, while from the right came the thunderous echo of native drums and the shouts of men and women. The whole place was impressive enough by itself, but to add to everything imagine a little road winding between the massive boulders, now clinging for footing on the edge of the envious krantzes, and now blasted and torn from the rocky grip of the very hill itself; and so coming out hundreds of feet above, on the wind-swept plateau of Mysinyanga.

We camped in a deserted roadworker's hut, and were comfortably settling down for supper when I discovered an army of little grey insects ascending my boots. There are insects and creepy things of all kinds, but for sheer unpleasantness the jigger, or *matakenya*, is the most noted. This little crawling flea burrows into one's skin and lays a vast abundance of eggs, which, if allowed

---

[1] *Umtasa, or Mutasa or Mafambá-Busuku, chief of the Nica tribe, which gives its name to Manicaland. The treaty between him and Archibald Ross Colquhoun (afterwards the first Administrator of Mashonaland), on behalf of the Chartered Company, was signed 14 September, 1890.*

[2] *A narrow pass between precipitous hills or mountains.*

to hatch, mean ten days in hospital. I pointed them out to Mr. Leckie Ewing, who thought we might escape invasion by laying our blankets on some old sheets of galvanized iron which stood about, and raising the iron on logs and stones. This would give us a pair of impromptu beds.

Some men say that pumpkins, others that feather beds, are the most uncomfortable things to sleep on; but I think that galvanized iron, with one thickness of blanket underneath, is bad enough for most. And as this thought began to take hold on me, I heard a scuffling in the grass roof and around the walls. I could see nothing. Leckie Ewing travelled sumptuously, that is to say he had brought a candle, but we had blown it out. The scuffling noise became louder every moment; suppressed squeaks rose above the incessant rustling, and tiny feet ran lightly across my blankets.

Mr. Leckie Ewing's voice, tense with subdued excitement, broke the hubbub.

'What the dickens is making all that noise?' he demanded.

Before I could reply there was an agonized yell, and I heard the composer of oratorios dive under his blanket.

'Poof! by heaven—' his voice was thick with woven wool—'a rat fell on my face! A rat by gad! For Heaven's sake strike a match—I can't find any!'

A few moments of hurried fumbling in the haunted depths of the skoff-box, and I struck a light. A scene, the like of which men see in dreams alone, met our horrified gaze. Rats leaped from the skoff-box—from under our galvanized beds—from under our very noses. They rushed into cracks in the walls, and so great was the crush that they sometimes jammed; they sped up the walls in strings: big ones—too big to be described—little ones and ones of middle size. They sprang on to us and over us, squealing like demons. Multitudes fought and struggled in the thatched roof. Here and there were holes to which they tore; at one hole there was a block, and a whole writhing phalanx of clinging rats, of all sizes and every degree of horribleness, dropped shrieking to the floor.

In ten seconds it was all over, and we two were left staring at each other with white faces. We laughed till we were on the verge of hysteria, but when we looked at the mangled remnants of our candle, at the skoff-box from which every atom of untinned food had been taken, and at one ripped boot, we had another feeling in our hearts besides that of amusement. I knew a man at Massikessi who, weakened by fever and lack of food, had to battle for his very life against the famished pigs of his own farm-yard. His companion, even weaker and more ill than himself, was dragged by the pigs from his bed not two yards away, and eaten alive. . . . I felt that I should not like to be a sick man left with that army of rats.

The next day we rose to the Mysinyanga level— a plateau of cold breezes and short grass where we saw khnoorhaan [1] and secretaries, two birds that I always associate with that veld—just as I learned, later on, to associate swimpey [2] with Urungwe, guinea-fowl with the valley of the Zambesi, bush pheasants with the lower Sabi, and dikkop [3] and peewits with Rusapi. Before us,

---

[1] ' Scolding-cock,' the common bustard.

[2] From the Zulu in-Swempe, a quail, the name given to the Bush partridge.

[3] A Dutch name for the stone plover.

but many miles away, loomed the massive outline of the Mountains of the Moon.

At midday Mr. Leckie Ewing left me at my father's property, and went forward towards Inyanga, his eyes full of eagerness. . . .

My boys and I camped on a little neck of land, the narrowest strip of the plateau, and began building the hut; but first of all we put up a temporary shelter, just large enough to sleep in at night, and here a strange thing happened. We were asleep, a fire burning in the middle of the little hut; presently I was aroused by a gentle movement. Several strange Kafirs were in the hut, one was making up the fire; my own boys were sleeping like logs. The Kafirs looked at me, and with perfect assurance took the blanket that covered me, they then rolled me over and took my under-blankets. They took my rifle, my boys' blankets, clothes, and food, and quietly went away.

Of course I thought I was dreaming, though I had never before dreamed of Kafirs—nor, indeed, have I since. But the curious fact is that I was not dreaming! We all awoke at dawn, bitterly cold, to find rifle, food, blankets —almost everything we possessed—gone !

I turned on my boys with an explosion of language that would have done credit to one of maturer years.

' Where are our things ? ' I asked.

In their naked chilliness they looked sheepishly at me and at one another. Then one of them remembered.

' Magondo ! ' he exclaimed, ' I saw the men take my things ! '

Then we all remembered, and that put a stop to recriminations. We did not attempt to discuss the mystery, but went forth armed with sticks and axes—the latter had been stuck in the thatching and had been overlooked. We tracked the thieves for several miles, but at length lost the spoor. We were as savage a little party as could well be imagined; had the thieves fallen into our hands, I believe we should have brained them, and hacked them limb from limb.

We returned furiously disconsolate. My boys considered that we had been bewitched—every one of us remembered perfectly well seeing the strange Kafirs enter our shelter and quietly take our belongings; but that we should have remained quiescent, and have returned to peaceful slumbers, seemed a thing marvellous beyond imagination.

We found that enough food was left to enable us to stay a few more days; this we did, and completed the hut, but every night we took turns in mounting guard. I greatly regretted that I had left Vixen behind at Hygeia.

And when the work was done we went back, making a long trek of twenty-six miles in the day. Three almost naked boys and myself—dressed in pyjamas, a pair of boots, and a turban of dirty calico—arrived by night at Hygeia and told our story. We were received with entire incredulity, though the fact of our nakedness was patent to all.

Years afterwards a great number of rifles, and a quantity of other stolen goods, were discovered in a kraal at Mysinyanga. The Native Commissioner told my father that he had heard of other cases like mine. His theory was that certain natives knew of a herb, which

when thrown on a fire gave off a smoke that had a drug-
ging effect upon the senses. He quite believed my
adventure, and thought that our thieves had either
thrown the herb on our fire while we slept, or made
a small fire outside up-wind, so that the smoke blew
through the thin thatching of our little shelter. I think,
to-day, that he was right.

VII

I SURVEY RUSAPI

Gone are those resolute trekkers—pilgrims who passed through
    the desert ...
Suns no longer shall smite them, nor ever the moon enchant! ...
Stern was the conflict and long, but the desert has broken and
    crushed them . . .
Merged are they in its fabric—one with the infinite veld!

FRANCIS CAREY SLATER.

(*The Karoo.*)

SOON after this a number of farms and a township in
the district of Rusapi required surveying. I went as my
father's advance agent for the purpose of building survey
beacons on all the kopjes for five miles or so around
Carr's store on the Rusapi—or Lesapi—River. I walked
the distance, sixty odd miles, following the survey line
of the Mashonaland Railway. At the Odzi, Inyazura, and
Inyamapamberi rivers the bridge builders had started
work. At various points on the survey line were contractors' huts, where great gangs of Kafirs—ranging from
the Mabandawi of the Lakes to the clean-built fighting
men of Matshanga—were digging the cuttings and laying
down the embankments of the permanent way.

'Chai-ire!'[1] called the overseers; and a hundred
hungry voices would respond in chorus, 'Hara-hara!'[2]

[1] '*Chai-ire!*' or '*chia-ele*', *it has struck (i. e. noon has struck,
therefore it is time to cease work and eat*).
[2] '*Hara-hara!*', *Hurrah.*

I camped with strange men at night, and heard strange speech and tales. Some of the men had worked on the Beira railway—you knew them by their yellow faces—but most of them came from England or the Argentine. This high-veld work was a different matter from the here-to-day-and-gone-to-morrow struggle on the Pungwe Flats, but even here men died. I remember Robinson, a florid, jovial man who told us all about his wife and three little children in a London suburb—whither he was returning when his contract was over. He had calculated that he would make good money; he showed me his assets and his liabilities, and where he saved while other men drank. Before I returned the Head Overseer had come that way by night, calling 'Chai-ire' as he passed. And Robinson had put by his figures and his tools, leaving an address for his last cable home.

The man who sent that cable was my friend Hutchinson, at that time working for my father; and he too has gone. And Dicky Marks, the mason; and his chum Angus. And Bloech of Transau and Ross of Rusapi. And the merry Irish lad at Inyazura, and the bridge-builder at the Odzi, and many another of whose hospitality I partook, whose names I have forgotten, but whose faces are still in my eyes. *Hara-hara!* my brothers, we may yet meet again.

A lad of thirteen, dressed in knickers and shirt sleeves, I walked on the outskirts of the Empire, where the shouting of men, the ring of hammers on stone, and the thud of picks in the baked earth were always in my ears. I saw the dust blow from the rising embankments, and the rocks rent asunder in the cuttings. Fig and thorn and kafir-orange vanished before the axes; villages of grass and canvas sprang to life amidst the virgin veld. Men sang along the flanks of mountains, within whose caves the forgotten Bushman had painted his gallery of beast and tree and battle. The little streams did not know themselves; perspiring bodies gloried in their crystal clearness where, perchance, men had never washed before. The long brown grass yielded her crop of thatch. The stone faces of the sleepy kopjes were rent with dynamite, that the bridges of the British people might be established in security. The wild bees were pestered by a score of thieves. The baboons shouted at the intruders; the horned game fled westwards to the Sabi.

And so I went ahead on the tide of progress, wondering and observing, and thinking of the thousand homesteads that would some day dot these fields.

It was spring. Over the granite kopjes of the high-veld came the lichens in lovely tints of ivory and red and yellow. The umsasas clustered round the giant rocks were a delicate intricacy of every shade from crimson to opal brightness. Scorpions and centipedes deserted their winter quarters under stone and bark; and every evening the long-tailed night-jars flitted noiselessly before us as we returned to camp. Sand-veld is merry veld, and we had a good time at Rusapi notwithstanding certain inconveniences.

The inconveniences were in the matter of food. My father had given me two or three pounds, and expected to join me at Rusapi in the course of about a week. I spent the money at Carr's store on ufu for my boys and bully beef and canned fruit for myself. But my father was delayed, and did not arrive for a month or more. In the course of the first fortnight I ran out of provisions, and a curious diffidence prevented me from buying further supplies 'on tick', so I ate ufu—plain, unappetizing ufu made from ropoko.[1]

The bridge contractor and Carr himself several times invited me to dinner, but the pride of poverty had taken root in my heart, and only once did I leave my own camp fire. On that occasion I ate enormously of boiled fowl, notwithstanding my efforts to check my appetite, and went away resolutely determined not to go again. I had not taken a gun, so I had no way of potting the few orebi that sped before us over the plains, or the sparse dikkop that bobbed their heads at us. Rusapi is high, open country, wide grass plains dotted here and there with granite kopjes. My two boys and I armed ourselves with knobkerries, and sometimes, on our way home from the day's work, we would have an impromptu game drive. We would approach a likely looking glade from different sides, and I would put Vic in to rouse the orebi. Our intention was to brain the orebi as it rushed out. But orebi are not so easily caught. Never did we get within a hundred yards of one.

We were more successful with the native fish-traps. My boys used to visit these early in the morning, and I am ashamed to say I did not scorn to share the two or three miserable little sardines that were only too seldom the reward of their dishonesty. There were no guinea-fowl to snare, no pheasants, no cane-rats, not even an oily lagevaan.[2] For a long time field-mouse was the only flesh we tasted. At sundown we used to dig the little animals from their earths. 'Sixpence', the picannin, would dig away with a pointed stick, while Vic, and the

[1] *Maize.*   [2] *Iguana.*

other boy—Simon—and I would wait around and keep a sharp look-out lest our quarry should escape by another exit. Sometimes we bagged three or four in the evening. We cooked them very simply—putting them straight on the burning embers, and when the hair had frizzled off and they looked cooked, we disembowelled them. If we had first skinned them, there would have been nothing left.

Sixpence was a pimply and bandy-legged youth with a great store of unedifying tales about life in his native Senna. Simon came from farther north, and was professedly a Christian; he belonged to the tribe of Mabandawi, of whom vast numbers have been Christianized by the Blantyre missionaries. He carried a small ' Reader ' of a religious nature. From this book with some difficulty he could make out a few monosyllabic sentences. Even these became fewer in the unacademic atmosphere of Rusapi.

Simon was a flagrant braggart. One of his favourite utterances was that nothing could make him afraid. But he was obviously terrified of Vic, and when we pointed this out to him he admitted that, as a matter of fact, he did have an instinctive objection to dogs. He fell further in our estimation by taking to his heels while Sixpence and I were robbing a native hive. He explained this by saying that it was dishonest to steal honey, and moreover stolen honey was sure to give one a stomach ache—' for the owners of the hive have buried magic at the foot of the tree.' On the same day we tried to scale a kopje known as the Lion's Head, in order to build a beacon on the summit. The kopje had been fortified against the Matabele or the Tshangaans by the Makalanga of old. We had to crawl on all fours through a narrow stone gateway. No sooner had we all emerged than we became aware of a vast rock-python coiled amidst the fallen rocks of the upper side, and regarding us with a beady stare. We were all startled, for we must have passed within a few inches of the creature; but Simon was so thoroughly horrified that infection was transmitted to the picannin and myself, and we made no effort to kill the reptile. After this we discovered the skulls of several deceased baboons, which pointed to the prowess of the rock-python, and Simon became dubious about the advisability of proceeding up the kopje. He advised a swift descent by another route, saying that the place was bewitched. However, we reassured him, and came at length to the base of an immense boulder that crowned the summit. The boulder was rent in two parts, and was capped by a smaller. Up this rent I sent Simon, while Sixpence and I waited till the passage was clear.

It became clear sooner than we expected. As Simon put his face over the upper ledge, he uttered a piercing yell and, tumbling down the rent, fled helter-skelter and shouting down the kopje. His terror was so complete that his black face, as he dashed past me, appeared positively blanched—and this apparent whitening of the face is no exaggeration, for I have seen other Kafirs in a like state.

Sixpence and I, drawing clear of whatever demon guarded the summit of the boulder, sat down and roared with laughter; but I do not think either of us was feeling any too steady. I know that at length, when I faced the rent myself, I took my sheath knife naked between my teeth and made the ascent in a very leisurely manner. As I raised my head warily over the ledge I found myself looking into the cold eye and at the blunted nose and flicking tongue of a python at least twice—so it seemed to me—the length, girth, and potency of the one by the rocky gate!

Without further ado I lowered myself from that position of danger, and Sixpence and I joined Simon on the plain below—when the latter carefully explained to us that the missionaries had warned him more than once of the iniquity of snakes.

About this time we proposed erecting a new beacon on a hill called Commonage Kop. It was fortified, like the Lion's Head, with several lines of stone walls. When we had surmounted these we came upon the real difficulty. Upon our left towered a mighty granite monolith, quite unscaleable; at our feet was a crevasse—a great rent in the granite, of profound depth and hideous aspect; before us, and separated from us by the crevasse, was another monolith crowned with a ring of boulders—the citadel of the fortification. The monolith upon our left, which was the highest point, was coped with an immense boulder, and could be reached only by surmounting Menhir No. 2. From Menhir No. 2 clung perilously an ancient and decrepit pole, over which, no doubt, some one had once essayed to reach the sky-supporting crest of Menhir No. 1.

A yawning chasm lay before us, and this could be crossed only by the aid of long stout poles set against the slippery face of Menhir No. 2. But the thought of creeping across another wobbly pole afterwards, and at a still greater altitude, sent a cold shiver down my back. The nervousness of Simon was quite comforting to witness. We all three sat down (in order to get a surer purchase on terra firma) to discuss the situation, and fixed our eyes on the ancient pole that hung fifty feet above us. It was an extraordinary coincidence, but seemed to us fraught with a horrid significance, that at that very moment the ancient pole slipped, lost its balance, and hurtled directly down the crevasse to fall with a sickening crash a hundred feet below. I flung myself a yard or two back. A grey smile of horror pulled wryly at the pimpled face of Sixpence. Simon merely groaned and rolled over on his face, grasping convulsively at the lichened granite. Even Vic was moved, and, deserting the alluring entrance of a badger hole, peered shiveringly over the rent.

As soon as I felt sufficiently recovered I ordered the two boys to go down to the plain and cut a long stout pole, but Simon hysterically declined to take any part in the surmounting of either of the massive menhirs, and declared that this place—the gloomy, yawning chasm—was very much like the ' Hell-o ' of whose torments the Blantyre missionaries had frequently spoken.

Not altogether ungrateful to the missionaries, I determined to leave Commonage Kop to my father. A week or two later he turned up, accompanied by his assistant, Cadoux. We thus changed our frugal diet for plenteous boiled fowl, rice, sweet potatoes, and tinned stuff. I told my father of the difficulties of Commonage Kop, and we set off there at once taking a good supply of rope and axes. Simon absented himself for the day. When we arrived at the foot of the great monoliths it struck me that I was feeling a good deal bolder than before; and for the first time I realized that confidence is catching.

We cut long poles, lashed them together, and laid

them against Menhir No. 2. We took off our boots and climbed up, one by one. Then we hauled up two more poles and laid them across the abyss. The far ends of them rested unsteadily on the edge of Menhir No. 1 at an upward angle. Upon the summit was the great boulder, upon the top of which my father proposed to set up his theodolite and take observations. All round the base of the boulder, between it and the monolith, was a narrow ledge overlooking the gulf. It was proposed to crawl round this ledge to the other side, from which it appeared that the big boulder might be climbed. My father was for going first, to reconnoitre the position, for he was a fearless man. But Cadoux would not let him, and insisted on a picannin being sent first with a rope, for the smaller the climber the better chance of life he would have on that narrow ledge. My father had a picannin, but he promptly prostrated himself on the rock, and refused to budge. So finally my poor pimply Sixpence was selected. We roped him well, and sent him off. It was hair-raising to see the poles wobble. Four boys tried to steady them, while the rest of us payed out Sixpence's life-line. He passed the poles in good style, and wormed his way agonizingly round the narrow ledge: but once in safety on the far side his spirit failed him, and we could hear him sobbing aloud, ' *Yowe, maiwango - maiwango - we !* ' (' Alas, my mother, my mother !')

Then my father went across, and then Cadoux ; and they set up the theodolite, and took their observations. But I remained on the top of Menhir No. 2 ; in the first place because I was not wanted on the boulder, and in the second place because I would not have made the journey if I had been. And when they made the return journey

I found that Cadoux, too, was a brave man. He was a Londoner, and could not be expected to have much experience of places like Commonage Kop ; but, my father and he being the last to make the descent, he insisted that my father should precede him. So that he himself crossed the two poles with no one at the farther end to hold them steady.

When we were at length on solid earth again, I had a narrow escape from losing my life. I was standing at the foot of the second monolith from which the boys were coming down one by one. My back was towards the monolith, and my father and Cadoux were standing about fifteen yards away across a little crevasse and facing me. Suddenly I became aware of a dull, gritting noise, and glancing towards my father I saw him gesticulating wildly and struggling to speak.

‘ Look out ! ’ shouted Cadoux ; and I drew back into the hollow base of the monolith.

On the same instant a great boulder, that must have weighed five hundredweight, crashed from the monolith above and splintered into a thousand fragments upon the very spot where I had been standing.

One of the boys on the summit had set the great stone sliding down the monolith, not knowing that I was standing just below. My father reached over to a forked shrub and seized his rifle ; and the boy who set that stone a-sliding came very near to following it. But even as my father opened the breech-block he changed his mind, and putting down the rifle again said quietly :

‘ That was a narrow squeak, old Turnip-top ! ’

VIII

TOWARDS THE SABI

Paint her as Naiad—nymph of fount or spring
And many a river's urn—
Whence waters outpour'd—east or westward turn!
Sanyati and Ngezi—gathering
Sebwakwe to them—own thy motherhood :
She cradles Sabi's ocean-reaching flood.

ARTHUR SHEARLY CRIPPS,
(*Charter-Country.*)

JOHANNES STEPHANUS MARITZ—to whom I have already referred—was a nephew of the Gerrits Maritz who, with Piet Retief, gave his name to Pietermaritzburg. He had come to Manicaland in the early days, about 1888 I think. No one knew where he came from; my father thought from Barberton, but Maritz himself told me that he had seen Lord Chelmsford's column pass his father's farm not long before it was annihilated at Isandhlwana. So I knew he came from Natal.

Maritz was Dutch by descent but he was loyal to England. I never heard him speak a word of Taal, but he was a fine linguist in Cheswina. He was a power among the Maswina, understood them and knew how to curse them into a state of prostration. I do not mean to say that Maritz was a foul-mouthed man ; he was very far from it. I never heard him swear in English; he was very different from the English store-keepers, contractors, and mining men. But in speaking Cheswina he entered into the spirit of the people.

He was a very tall man, six foot three I should think, with

H

a beaked nose and fierce, grey eyes. He was taciturn, and had no friends; but he seemed to like me, and often told me stories when we were alone together. Other people told me stories about him too—one that he never told himself was about the Mashona rebellion. The English people at Old Umtali, when the rebellion broke out, were afraid that Umtasa would join in to murder and ravage like the rest of the Maswina. It was known that Maritz was an Induna of Umtasa's kraal, he had been given this honour for some reason I did not know, and Umtasa used to send him presents of cattle, ivory, and fat-tailed sheep. The people of Umtali thought he might influence the chief, so Maritz rode twelve miles to his kraal, went in alone and unarmed, and prevailed upon him not to start war in Manicaland. This saved us from what might have been a massacre of six or seven hundred men and women, or at best a hard fight against tremendous odds. Nevertheless, two or three years later Maritz was arrested because he became bankrupt and had not kept account books. I remember that when I heard the news I went out alone on the veld, to work off my indignation.

Maritz's stories of the veld interested me tremendously. He told them very slowly, sometimes putting out his long brown hand in emphasis. He had a lean, weatherbeaten face, rather like a tortoise, and his fierce eyes used to pick up points on the blue horizon as if he had spent his life wandering into strange lands. Buffalo— lions—elephants—he knew all the things of the veld. He had killed them and often been nearly killed by them. He did not speak *about* the veld animals, but he spoke *of* them—as a man speaks of loved and familiar things.

The names of places when he used them seemed to live in one's mind. 'The Flats'—'the Gold Belt'—'the Crocodile'—'the Sabi'—all these names used to run in my head for weeks after listening to him. I liked 'The Sabi' specially. He had a way of pronouncing this simple name that just made you see the blue water flowing amongst the worn boulders. In my mind's eye I pictured the great river with huge trees on its banks, and elephants drinking at sundown. I could see the crocodiles lying on the sand-spits, and the swirl of gigantic barbel in spring-time.

So you will guess how glad I was when my father said he was going down to the Sabi to do some surveying. I went with him, also Fiennes Taylor, his assistant, and a Mr. Palmer whose land required surveying.

We slept the first night at Bloech's farm, fifteen miles from Umtali ; the next day we crossed the Odzi river, and, following the Gold Belt, we camped at a water-hole about eleven miles from Bloech's farm. The next morning, alas, I awoke ill and tired, and they decided that I had a touch of fever. So I was given a boy to carry my blankets and was sent back ignominiously to Umtali.

A few days of bed and quinine, however, set me on my feet, and I told my mother I was going down to the Sabi to find Dad. She lent me another native servant, and with him and the boy who had carried my blankets I set out.

I started down our little kopje and faced the great veld with much exhilaration. It was no small venture for a lad of twelve. Eight miles from Umtali I would pass a wayside store ; seven miles on I would come to Bloech's ; another five miles and I would come to the Odzi river

where the bridge builders were hard at work in anticipation of the Mashonaland Railway. Beyond this there
was neither road nor house; for the next thirty, forty—
or as I thought fifty—miles I would tramp westwards,
never seeing a white man, but following winding paths
that led amongst the hills. I would follow the setting sun
until I struck the Sabi river, and would then go north
until I came to the junction of the Tsungwesi. I would
follow this up on the south bank till I found my father;
for he told me he meant to camp on the near bank of
the Tsungwesi. The whole distance was not so great
as I thought, but, allowing for the devious paths, it was
well over sixty miles, and every mile of it held possibilities. At any turn of the path I might come face to face
with a lion, and then I would have to kneel and shoot
straight—my life depending on it. Or I might walk
right into a herd of elephants. Worse still, a leopard
might leap our frail *scherm* [1] at night and drag off and eat
one of my boys.

As a matter of fact none of these things happened,
but we fell on an adventure that I shall never forget. We
avoided the store and the farm and the bridge, and slept
every night under the stars. It was a little lonely in the
evenings, but Vic sat beside me and was very comforting.
Beyond the Quagga water-hole, where previously I had
been taken ill, the path turned southwards, skirted the
hill called 'Frank Johnson', and took us to a cluster of
native huts and Kafir gardens beyond Nyarugwi Peak.

We spent the night in an empty grain hut in some
Kafir gardens, and I discovered that a very good dish

[1] *Screen, generally made of branches of trees (Dutch* scherm,
a screen, fence).

may be made of fried onions and bully beef. Next morning we followed the directions of the natives, and came late in the afternoon to the last kraal my father had visited. At this kraal the natives seemed peculiarly foolish; we could get no information whatever from them. When I asked a group of men who were collected round the village fig tree which way the white men had gone, they looked at one another and repeated the question. Then I inquired if the white men had been there at all. Some thought they had, some thought they hadn't, and a lively discussion began.

The situation was saved by a thin little old lady, nearly naked, who pushed unceremoniously through the group and walked boldly up to me. She had the pleasantest face imaginable, withered and sunburnt, but covered with merry lines and lit with a cheery smile. Her forehead was smooth and open, and her chin high in the air. Walungu, the white men? Yes, of course they had been there. Ai! Ai! what were the old men talking about? There were three Walungu—one with a beard. Yewohe! So that was my father? They had gone so—she pointed with her lively hand towards the north-west— and they were not far. To-morrow, if I started at sunrise, I would find them at the Tsungwesi, ' *dzua radai* '[1]— she indicated with her hand where the sun stood at four o'clock.

The old lady lent us her own hut for the night, and I thanked her as well as I could, calling her ' Mother '. She chatted with us for a long while, and I wished I could have understood all that she said, but neither I nor my boys (who belonged to a different tribe) could follow

[1] ' *Dzua* ', *the sun* ; ' *radai* ', *was or is there,* or ' *like that* '.

her very well. She warned us that there was no path and not much water to be had, but she gave us instructions where to find a water-hole. Altogether she was delightfully keen and intelligent, and since then I have often noticed, both amongst the blacks and our own people, that old women are far brighter and wittier than elderly men.

We started out at sunrise and followed the path. Before we had gone many hundred yards I heard a gentle ' pad-pad-pad ' and, peering through the bushes, I saw a huge baboon. He was a mighty fellow, brown and hairy and terrible of aspect. I whispered to the boys to wait, and went carefully ahead till I could get a clear shot. The bullet could not have missed him by more than an inch, and I saw the dust and grasses move where it struck. But the old man neither started nor looked back; he just stepped off the path and walked heavily on to the red and yellow lichens of a great granite boss. The boss sloped gently upwards from the path for a great distance and ended in a shaggy kopje. I followed him on to the rock and fired again ; I was no more than forty yards away. He sat down and looked at me. I fired once more and the Martini bullet screamed off the granite. He lifted one of his hands, looked away from me at the veld around, put down his hand and walked quietly on.

So I went back to the path. A little farther on it swung to the south, and we struck off north-west into the scrub. It was lonely country, having no sign of man or game. We crossed many dongas, but there was no water in them—only white sand, and boulders rounded by the floods of summer.

At noon we heard two shots away on our right, and a

few minutes later saw the smoke of a grass fire rising into the clear air. At top speed we hurried to the place, but when we came there the fire had already spread widely, and whoever had lit it was gone. There was nothing to be seen but the yellow fire licking up the withered grass, and nothing to be heard but the roar of it, and the cries of bij-fangers[1] and blue jays as they darted through the smoke to catch flying insects. We turned left again and tramped steadily on through the catching thorns and the hot air.

A little later I called a halt. Since there was no water with which to cook my boys' *sadza*, I opened two tins of bully beef, and shared this with them. Bully beef is very salt, and on a blazing day with not a breath of cool air or a drop to drink it gives one an agonizing thirst; I think this meal was accountable for some of our troubles. Anyhow my two boys began to malinger. Their loads wanted re-tying; for this purpose they stripped off the bark of young umsasas, and they chewed some of the bark. They were for ever getting thorns in their feet, and each thorn meant an indefinite stop. At short intervals they got tired, and asked for a rest—in fact it was hard work to keep them moving at all. Once or twice we searched a dry donga for a mile up and down; but the dongas held nothing but sand and stones.

At about five o'clock we came on a deserted camp; a few old huts, some fallen in, some twisted and awry. We passed over some grass-grown cuttings and found a shaft. The windlass had been eaten by white ants, and the windlass barrel, riddled with borers, lay across the mouth. A battered claim peg stood near by, and its black

[1] *The bee-catcher, called in Natal the smoke-bird.*

lettering, peeled by the sun, indicated the position, owner, and the reef's name: THE DAY DAWN. We all three lay down on the crumbling edge of the shaft and dropped stones in; it was nice hearing them splash into deep water, sixty feet below.

The boys had had enough. 'Mlungu,' they said (those were the days when they called one 'Child of the Sky'), 'We will go no farther.'

I swung my rifle from my shoulder to my left hand and stepped aside to let them pass.

'Go on,' I said, 'or I will shoot you.'

They passed on without a word, and I followed behind. Neither of them spoke again, and so we came at dusk to the summit of a little hill.

The west, where the Sabi flowed, was lit with the last streamers of light. Darkness lay thick and silent among the hills, and crept towards us from the east.

I moved a few paces from the boys and fired rapidly, three times, into the air. It is the African signal of distress. The three flashes tore into the dark and blinded me; the noise seemed terrific. I strained every nerve to catch an answering shot, but in a few seconds the great silence closed in around us again, and I heard nothing but the blood drumming in my ears. My boys sat motionless with their faces between their knees, and their hands crossed above their heads.

I felt something hot stealing down my cheeks, and I gulped. The disappointment was too bitter.

'Come on,' I said, 'let us go back.'

They picked up their loads, and all that night we stumbled through the darkness. At dawn we arrived at the kraal where the old woman lived, and we drank and slept.

Next day by great good luck we fell in with one of my father's Kafirs, who had been sent for stores. He knew a shorter route to the Tsungwesi, and I ordered him to return and guide us. We came at sundown to the little camp, and behold! it was but a short two miles from where I had fired my distress signal two nights before! Now my father had taught me the African distress signal —the three shots fired rapidly—and if he had heard them it was his duty to reply with one shot.

'Surely you heard me fire?' I asked.

'Oh yes,' said my father lightly, 'but I thought it was Palmer after game.'

Such a flood of bitter indignation swept over me, that I sat silent and trembling, quite unable to speak. I could not forgive my father for his thoughtless indifference in not answering my shots, nor for his faulty veld-craft in not distinguishing between game shots and a signal— for it was nearly dark at the time, and no sane man would have been hunting; moreover, Palmer had left camp early in the morning, and by that time would have been twenty miles away.

Bitterness, however, was soon overlaid with interest, for the next afternoon I shot my first head of big game.

A Shangaan and I were climbing a hill, bent on the serious work of erecting a survey beacon and clearing the bush around it to make it visible from neighbouring peaks. Suddenly a rustle swept up the hillside before us, like the rustle of a whirlwind among dead leaves. In- stinctively, we both crouched to the ground.

'Inkoos,[1] inyama!'[2] whispered the Shangaan.

I stood slowly upright to command a better view.

[1] *Kafir* in-Kosi, *a chief.*   [2] Inyama, *game, food.*

Curiously, out of the maze of leaves and stones and brown trunks, something moved; it was the twitching ear of a cow waterbuck. Since then I have seen many a wild thing fall and struggle in the dust for having given way to that weakness—a twitch of the ear! I slowly raised the rifle and fired; there was a thud and crash, and the whirlwind swept on up the hill—but the old cow remained.

The exultation of one's first head of big game is a thing that stays; but on that day, and ever afterwards, though I have shot my food in many a wild place, I felt a keen sadness in the event. Far better, I thought, to have a great veld park where one might collect the beautiful antelope and get to know them intimately in other ways than by the fierce veld custom—which is 'stalk and kill'.

This old cow taught me another lesson also; for I thought we would have waterbuck tongue on the menu next morning. I fried the tongue—a fatal mistake; smaller and smaller it grew in the pan, till at length, having decreased to the size of an amorphous pellet, and having taken on the consistency of a ball of rubber, it was given to Vic. Vic, being of a courteous and obliging nature, accepted the delicacy; and hid it carefully behind a bush.

That night I heard old Tika, the hyena, for the first time, close at hand. The hyenas were attracted by the meat, and their savage 'Hur-hur' and blood-curdling 'Who-o-ee' made darkness a place of terror. Vic had not the slightest objection to hyenas, and, after listening to the hubbub for a few minutes, curled up again for sleep; but with lions and leopards it was otherwise. I have heard Vic dog a leopard at night—he had taken toll in the shape of a prize pointer—till her frenzied barks were out of earshot. And a whiff of lion—that whiff which sends most dogs howling to heel—stirred her Amazonian bosom to a ferocious chase. Alas, the African code is a hard one, death follows at the heels of virtue, and years afterwards my little Vic, old, blind, and worn in the tooth, met her end at the iron paw of Ingwi, the leopard. But Vic was then in the prime of her passionate life—keen on the scent, warm-hearted, and a bitter hater of all black skins.

The next day Dad and I put up a solitary sable bull. These lonely bulls are big and savage; too old to serve the herd, they are expelled by the rising generation and wander forth to concentrate their failing energies on a grim struggle for existence. Hunters say that after lions, elephants, and solitary buffalo, the wounded sable is the most dangerous beast, especially the solitary bull.

The old bull cantered athwart us, flicking in and out among the shadows, and crashing among the dead maj-anji leaves. Dad and I both fired, and both thought we had hit. Vic dashed forward along the trail. I was for calling her back, and for patiently tracking the old bull along his spoor; for I liked having my conflicts and doing my kills quietly, without ostentation, without fluster. But Dad thought Vic would worry the old fellow and make him stand on the defence, and thus give us a speedy chance of coming on him again.

As we were trying to pick up the blood spoor, a mighty roar resounded through the bush. The roar was repeated with such ferocity and volume that we both concluded that it was a lion.

'It's a lion,' shouted Dad—'got our sable!'

The string of boys behind us were evidently of the same opinion, for with much jabber and no hesitation they started off in the opposite direction. Dad and I rushed towards the sound, leaping over the shrubs and tearing our bare arms on the red-plum and medlar bushes.

Beyond a dry gully flanked by a mighty ant-heap lay the bull sable. He was down on his front knee and the splintered bloody stump that a few minutes before had been his other knee. He still kept his hind feet, but his rump was streaked with blood. His glossy black back was dripping with sweat, and here and there ruffed up and clogged with dust, so he had evidently fallen once or twice. Fixed to his left ear, as tightly as a tick on a bullock's dewlap, was Vixen.

This must have been more humiliating than when old Inyamkwarati was expelled from the herd. His half-open mouth was flecked with foam and trembling with rage, and every now and then he gave vent to the terrific bellow that we had mistaken for a lion's roar. He swung his head from side to side with a short irresistible jerk that would have sent his long horns through a two-inch deal plank, but Vic was safe in the curve—the cruel points whizzed harmlessly a foot beyond her stumpy tail.

Humiliating as his position was, the old sable, struggling in the dust and blood, has left on my mind a picture of majestic dignity the like of which is seldom seen. He held his head indomitably aloft; no gleam of fear invaded his blood-shot eyes. Despite his wounds his every fibre quivered with passionate resistance, and as he saw us appear on the summit of the ant-heap, his fury redoubled. He quite forgot Vic; stiffening his neck and lowering his chin, so as to bring his horns into the position of attack, he struggled towards us. He stopped bellowing, and the hot morning quivered with his eager, challenging snorts. Dad sat down and levelled his rifle . . . the shot rang out, and, as if wakening from a furious dream, we saw that fierce bulk of energy collapse on the instant and sink limply on the sand.

IX

ON AN OFFICE STOOL

'First at the desk, there is his post; there he delighteth to be. His first ambition, as appeareth all along, is to be a good clerk. . . . His whole deportment is staid, modest, and civil. His motto is "Regularity".'

CHARLES LAMB (*The Good Clerk*).

SOON after our return from the Sabi my father advised me to join the staff of the Standard Bank ' to learn something about money'. I did learn something, but my entries were mostly on the debit side.

The transition from the wild free life which I loved to the monotony of clerking was full of irritation. The atmosphere was one of petty accuracy. The work was never hard, there was very little to do, and what there was seemed entirely unimportant.

Every morning I signed on, every evening 1 signed off. Between these two events I filed cheques, copied letters, did clearances with the Bank of Africa, and posted a ledger. The most trying part of the day was the pretence of working when there was no work to do. I used to take a few sandwiches with me, and these I ate in the quiet midday hour when the Bank was deserted. That hour from one to two always seemed long, and I dreamed of many things. Sometimes I watched Sarah, the Bank baboon. She was an ape of great size, and she hated all Kafirs, and would fly at them if they came within reach of her chain. During my time two were sent to hospital after but a second's encounter with her. In the earlier days Sarah had escaped, and had over-fed herself on uncooked rice from the premises of the Manica Trading Company. For some days she hovered between life and bursting, but finally her limit of expansion proved wider than that of the rice. On another occasion we all hurried out of the Bank to find Sarah apparently in the last stages of intoxication, carrying on a furious altercation with a group of excited niggers. Our Sarah sober was a match for a whole tribe of natives; but Sarah drunk must have the protection of Walungu, the Children of the Sky. We took her tenderly indoors and put her to bed, and within a few minutes she had fallen asleep grunting contentedly as strong white hands covered her with a bit of sacking. The explanation of her unusual excess was a simple one: Sarah had devoured the remnants of a packet of sugar-coated sleeping pills, which one of the staff had carelessly thrown within reach of her chain.

I joined the Bank at a salary, with allowances, of £100 per annum. This was soon raised to £112, and when the Boer War broke out, in 1899, when I had spent twelve months in the service, I was given an additional allowance of sixty pounds a year.

When the war started I was fourteen, and a paper was sent round town for the names of men willing to serve at the front. I and five others appended our names. But my people were anxious that I should not go because, I suppose, I was the only son. Also there was some talk at the Bank about my not being allowed to go, because I was bound to give them three months' notice before leaving. But I took no notice of these difficulties, and my name was sent with the others to the head-quarters of the force that Plumer was raising at Bula-wayo.

Shortly after this a notice came telling us to hold our-selves in readiness to proceed to the front, and that we were expected to supply our own horse, saddle, and rifle. Of horse and gear I had none ; but I had my own rifle, and the other men said that a horse could be got in Bulawayo. However, a few days later, after the victory of Talana Hill, a telegram came from Bulawayo which said that the Commander-in-Chief of Her Majesty's forces in Natal considered that no irregular troops would be required for the conduct of the war. That was the end of my military ambition for the time. A few months later the Commander-in-Chief changed his mind about irregular troops, but I think we six were rather sore about it. Our enthusiasm had been sadly damped by the curt refusal of our services, and the war gave promise of being a long drawn out affair, in which many months would be spent in the not very enthralling occupation of guarding communications. So of the original six only one went in the end. But scores of more persevering fellow townsmen gave up the sure billet and the safe bed, and travelled eight hundred miles to the west and south to the service of their country—many of them to add their names to the dusty files of the honourable dead. Now that I am older I very much regret that I was not among the men who fought under the flag of England.

My last few months at the Bank and my first months of market-gardening were my Slough of Despond. I had taken to smoking, too soon by seven years or so. I de-veloped a mania for buying new pipes and attempting to colour them; I say 'attempting', because I seldom was without a new pipe long enough to put a tan on the last one. I did not even prove myself fit to colour pipes.

I hated one or two of my fellow clerks—good fellows they must have been to put up with as much of my impertinence as they did. I was insolent to the officer commanding my squadron of the Southern Rhodesia Volunteers, and my name was struck off the rolls. This had not even the effect of making me ashamed.

I wrote an insolent letter to a woman whose cows used to trespass on my land, and a friend of hers gave me a hiding for my pains. I took the thrashing stoically, and then summoned him to the Police Court and obtained a conviction; he was a big man and I was a wisp of a boy.

In business matters I was not so backward as in affairs of the spirit. I did a sharp little stroke of trading by buying three cows for thirty-two pounds and selling them for sixty pounds.

Perhaps it stands to my credit that I broke myself of the habit of stammering. This hateful drawback came on me just before I entered the Bank, and it stuck to me till shortly before I left. The humiliation of it was an increasing bitterness to me, and the effort I made to throw it off—an effort that was at length successful—was of an intensity almost heroic. The hours I spent alone on the Commonage, reading aloud to Vic and the long grass!

I ate infinitesimally and read enormously at this period. I was just entering upon the pimply age and perhaps that accounted for some of my uncouthness. Moreover, I had a bad friend. But against this one bad friend I made two good friends. And of these two one is my good friend still. The other has in some way altered, so that our friendship of that time does not return to us when we meet.

When I first met my friend I had left the Bank and was devoting all my time to my market garden. One afternoon, as I was raking over a seed bed, a young stranger crossed the little stream, and, coming towards me, stood still for a short while, and then asked if I were Kingsley Fairbridge. He was strongly built, broad-shouldered, and slightly stooping. His powerful-looking hands hung slackly at his sides as if he never used them for any more strenuous purpose than brushing away flies. His face was particularly handsome and well-balanced, though rather heavy-featured, like the faces of the old-time Greeks, and his expression was dogged, aloof, and slightly contemptuous. He had the Greek short upper lip, and his mouth was drawn deeply down at the corners.

I took an instant dislike to him, as I did years afterwards to the man who became my best friend in England. But during the few weeks that followed our meeting, I had more than ample cause to alter my opinion, and, as the Fates willed it, my gradual friendliness warmed into an admiration and affection that I doubt not will last our lives. This man was James Morrell, a mining engineer. From him I learnt something of the reticence, the true-heartedness, the loyalty, the piety, the unswerving obedience to duty, the youthful outlook, the intolerance, the contempt for strangers, and the respect for friends, and a score more of the curious qualities that go to make up the best of the English. At times he suffered from a bitter silence. At others he was the most light-hearted and inconsequent of good fellows.

My market garden was not my only source of income at this time, but the tending of it was an unfailing interest. I knew nothing of horticulture but what I picked up from reading seedsmen's catalogues. But I always sowed the seed myself, and watched with the closest attention the development of the young plants, so that by degrees I came to know the conditions which seemed best to suit the various vegetables. I wonder can any man resist the fascination of a well-drilled line of young peas just showing above the ground? Or the voluptuous, flourishing beauty of a matronly cauliflower? Or a healthy series of Canadian Wonder beans, each standing vigorous and branching in its allotted space like an avenue of miniature oaks? There is a great joy in producing all those happy green things from the little brown seeds, and in tending their healthy development.

X

JAMES MORRELL

Have your keen eyes grown dim
Watching the camp-fires die ?
And is the white ash waste within your heart,
The sky
Unto the dead world's rim
Sombre with smoke ?
Is aught left of the great hope but dreams that start ?
And are your feet
Sick of the roads and all their dust and heat ?

In the autumn of 1900 I was very ill. About New
Year, working in my market garden, I caught fever. The
garden lay between two streams about five hundred yards
west of Utopia; I was there early in the morning and
late at night, turning up the soil, sowing and transplant-
ing vegetables, and seeing that the produce was got
ready for the early market on Wednesdays and Saturdays.

All February I was laid up in bed. Then I got better
and went to the garden again, but in a day or two I was
back in bed. This happened again and again throughout
March. In April I was tired of it all and no longer eager
to live. The long green grass, bending in the east wind,
irritated me furiously. The damp weather, when the
mists covered the Inyamutshura Range and blew in
tatters past the window, made me feel very cold. Our
house was built of rough stones, some of them partly
sized; the stones were a deep blue colour where they

had been chipped, their untrimmed faces were yellow, and the daga [1] cement between them was dull red. The whole colour was too dark. If the room had been papered with white paper, with some pink flowers and interesting pictures, it would have cheered me.

Early in April I was prepared to die. I think I should have died, but one morning, when all my people were out of the house, our cook brought me a telegram: 'Will you come to the Zambesi with me, starting Friday. Morrell.'

That was Monday. I got out of bed and put on my clothes. I felt very light on my feet, but with a little difficulty I reached the town. I wired back to Salisbury, 'Yes, I will come, leaving to-morrow.' At the railway station they told me that a goods train might leave that evening; I spent half the night waiting for it, but it never went. The next night, and Wednesday night, I did the same thing. On Thursday morning Rice and I caught a goods train. Rice was of the tribe called Matanga; his home was somewhere east of Nyanga. He was obstinate and not very clever, but he was faithful and trustworthy. He carried a bundle of four blankets —his own and mine—a pair of trousers, a couple of shirts, several pairs of socks, and two hundred rounds of ammunition. The clothes and cartridges were rolled inside the blankets; outside was tied a tin pot made of a small oil-drum. I carried my service Lee-Metford and two bandoliers.

I had been very near death. The pitiful weakness of long-protracted malaria had left me almost without hope.

---

[1] *Dagher (from Kaf. u-Daka, mud, mortar), mud, often mixed with blood and cow-dung and worked up into a sort of mortar.*

I wonder does my friend James Morrell know that he
saved my life at this time—for save it he did. The
thought of the Zambesi was like wine in my head. The
Zambesi of that date was not the resort of wealthy English tourists that it is now; there was, of course, no
railway to it, and it was in fact very little known. The
great district of Bazizulu, through which Morrell and
I passed, was on the maps a mere blank over which was
written 'Elephants and Thick Bush'. What a grand
sound it had for a boy of fifteen! Elephants, thought
I, and lions, and rhinos—by Jove, yes, life might be worth
living after all! Without an effort I shouldered aside
the miseries that had seemed to accumulate upon my
shoulders at the Bank, and which my market gardening
had failed to dissipate. Before me lay an adventure that
called for hardihood and resource. Who could tell what
wonders the future held! I was turning over a new leaf.
My feet would leave even the paths behind. I was nearing
the summit of the range beyond which lay I knew not
what, except that it was the wilderness, untrammelled
and untrod.

With what better companion than James Morrell
could I make my journey? There he was, at Salisbury
station, his massive shoulders and noble face marking
him off from other men. He, too, had been ill, and was
supposed to be in the Nursing Home when he was, in
reality, braving the cold night air to meet me. That
was like him. But he had, however, to return to the
Nursing Home, so that several days elapsed before we
set out.

A Cape cart and six mules took us the first stage of
our journey. A thousand dreams filled my head as the

cart moved off towards the north-west. The dust blew to leeward, and Oom Paul, James's bull-terrier, scampered beside.

James Morrell had four wagons of provisions and mining apparatus. Rice was sent on with them to Sinoia, and James and I followed in the Cape cart a few days later. We slept the first night on the Gwibi Flats, and it was very cold; but James gave me one of his two blankets. I woke several times during the night owing to the cold, and I noticed that James never moved; he lay perfectly quiet, on his back, with a rough stump under his neck for a pillow. He always slept like that, quite quiet, as if he were dead tired; but I think he was never really tired, because in camp he was at his work all day long—sampling, panning, surveying, and working out figures; while on the veld he would be up at dawn to wake the Kafirs, and was ready to start before we others were out of our blankets.

Sinoia was seventy-five miles by road from Salisbury. I had another touch of fever when we got there, and so I stayed at the wayside store and James went on with Paterson, his contractor, Massikessi Smith, and about forty Shangaan mine boys. They were making for Urungwe, one hundred and ten miles north by path. The same day the wagons set out and only Rice stayed with me.

The officers and men of Sinoia Police Camp, who came down very often for a meal and drinks at the store, amused me; they had many interesting tales, though some of them could not be printed. They were surprised when they heard I was going to the Zambesi. They said that Urungwe was a death-trap. A police camp had been stationed there for a year, but as all the men died during the wet season it had been abandoned.

Rice and I set out in the afternoon, about a week after James and the wagons. I walked in front with the rifle, and Rice followed behind carrying the blankets and a few days' food. Towards evening we skirted a range of hills, and just before sundown three klip-springer started out of the grass and boulders by the pathside and dashed for a neighbouring krantz. Klip-springer are pretty little fellows who get over the great granite rocks with extraordinary ease and speed; their coat is long, and is composed of spindle-shaped hairs, hollow inside—looking rather like small porcupine quills. They are easy to shoot, because when they reach the summit of a high boulder they always pause to look round.

I dropped one of them on the run, and we waited, quite still, for another shot. The remaining two darted up the hillside in sudden zigzag jumps, and, sure enough, when they reached the top of the krantz, the ram jumped on a boulder and faced round towards us. I fired, and he sprang forward over the krantz and fell far below amongst the grass and scrub.

Rice and I skinned and cleaned the two buck, and a couple of natives returning to Imbowe's kraal carried the meat. We slept at Imbowe's, and next morning I bargained with the two Kafirs that they should carry on our *impashla* till we caught up the wagons, for which I would give them one of the klipspringer. They said we should reach the wagons that night.

The path lay across a long vlei, and then wound over flat country through umsasa woods. Presently we came in view of another great vlei on the right, parallel to the footpath. What a grand country for farming, I thought; here was a home for white men—wood and grass and plough-land. There was no river through the vlei, but water could be got not far below the surface.

While I was thinking of these things, one of the Imbowe boys said ' Inyama !'—game—and we all stopped. A small herd of tsessabe were feeding far off in the vlei. It was a difficult stalk, because I had to leave the trees, and on the vlei itself were only small patches of grass—the rest having been burned.

I ' took-off ' behind a sugar bush, and having got among the patches of grass I did not raise my head again, but crawled with great patience on my hands and knees. In not less than half an hour I judged that the tsessabe were about one hundred and fifty yards in front, so I raised my head cautiously, holding the rifle ready. But the tsessabe were quite as far off as before, about twelve of them, all looking in my direction. They were the first of these antelope that I had seen, and I did not know their alert and suspicious nature, so I spent another hour or so crawling about that vlei. The freshness of the morning had passed off, and it is very hot when your face is only a foot from the ground and the sun blazes on your back; moreover, my shirt was full of irritating grass seeds and my hands were getting sore from being leant on in the burnt stubble. It is tiring, too, moving like a dog with a thorn in its foot—one hand being required for the rifle.

So after several failures I gave up the chase, and started back for the path. But the tsessabe had got disbanded by my manœuvres, and I came in sight of three of them standing behind a big ant-heap and looking towards me.

Only their heads and necks were showing, and they were about five hundred yards away, bunched together. I sat down and ' browned ' them, not expecting to hit, and the three tsessabe made off at a great pace. But suddenly my boys appeared from the bush, running towards the ant-heap. A lucky chance had directed my bullet, which had laid out a tsessabe cow—I had evidently miscounted the buck. We did not find the wound for some while, as she was hit between the eyes, and the mark scarcely showed on her deep red hide.

Rice and I stayed to skin, and the two Maswina went off to a neigbouring kraal to fetch men and women. They came late in the afternoon, and cut up the kill with their *mademo*—their home-made axes of soft iron. They did the work badly, mauling the meat and showing no knowledge of butchering ; only the Matshangaana, of all Rhodesian Kafirs, seem to understand the job. They carried in the meat, and I traded part of it for eggs, monkey-nuts, sweet potatoes, and ufu. By this time it was night, but the headman said the wagons were not far off, so we pushed on.

The wagons were badly stuck. As we reached the top of a low ridge we could hear the drivers and transport riders calling on their bullocks by name, straightening the spans, and then the swish and crack of their long whips. One of the wagons had been pulled out of the swampy edge of the vlei and was outspanned six hundred yards farther on ; the span, all except the two after-oxen, had been taken back and linked on to the fore-end of another span. The great strain now and again broke the iron links of the after-chain, and the work had to stop for repairs ; it was quite dark, so repairing was difficult.

The women and men put the tsessabe meat on the out-spanned wagon, and returned the same night to their kraal.

James Morrell, tired of the slow-moving wagons, had pushed on for Urungwe, taking with him Paterson, Smith, and the mine boys. Rice and I camped with the wagons, and had supper with the transport riders, one of whom was an Irishman named Short.

The next day we got two more wagons out, but the fourth was sunk to the axles. The water-cask was jammed underneath, and the brakes were clamped on to the after-wheels by the clinging mud. The bullocks did not feed at night, but were tied to the chains, because this big vlei and the whole valley of the Angwa river (which lay a few miles to the west) was lion country. The two wagons were got free and outspanned before breakfast; then the cattle went off to feed.

After breakfast we unloaded the sunken wagon. Then we dug in front of the fore-wheels and laid grass under them. But before the after-wheels had been loosened the mud silted in and choked the fore-wheels again—and I think they even sank a little deeper.

The sunken wagon was abandoned and its load distributed. The wagon-pole had been dragged out of its socket, the body was buried to the naves, and it looked very lonely on the wide veld as we turned away. There was no road, only a faint footpath and the track of a Cape cart which had been to Urungwe a year or two before. The wagon moved too slowly for me, so with Rice, and two boys who were returning to Mazimbagupa's kraal, I pushed on ahead.

We slept the next three nights on the veld, every evening cutting down big umsasa trees and piling them, branch inwards, for a *scherm* to keep out lions. We drew thorns and small bushes between the branches. We built our cooking fires some forty or fifty yards from the *scherm*, because the boys said that rhinos, seeing a fire at night, will rush in and stamp it out; and that is dangerous. One evening we crossed a stream, and the boys as they walked broke off little twigs and threw them into the water; there was a god in there, they said, who brought good or evil luck.

As we neared Mazimbagupa's kraal we came on a region of great vleis; the soil was rich and brown, very fertile, but we had seen neither man nor stock. The only signs of life were occasional glimpses of sable and tsessabe, great quantities of big game spoor, and at several points the spoor of lions and hyenas. As I was thinking of these things, I saw two men coming towards us, one of them carrying an open note fixed in a cleft stick. The note was in James Morrell's writing, and addressed to Mr. Short. I opened and read it. James said that food had given out, and he urged Mr. Short to hurry on the wagons.

I laughed when I thought of the wagons being hurried; they could not reach Urungwe for several weeks.

'Is there no game to shoot at Urungwe?' I asked.

And the boy said, 'There is no game'.

I gave him back the note and sent him on, and then I considered if it would not be better to stay where I was and leave the hungry camp to look after itself. But I remembered that James was not a very good shot nor accustomed to hunting his food, and I thought if I went on I could easily get enough food for us two at least— even if it were only lagevaans and rock-salamanders. Besides there must surely be kraals somewhere near

Urungwe, so it could only be a matter of discomfort and not real starvation.

Good luck walked with me that morning : we had not advanced more than a hundred yards before I sighted a great herd of game. They lay near the edge of a wood far away to our left. One of the boys said, *Inyamkwarati* (sable antelope), the other said they were roan antelope; but Rice maintained *Imbidzi* (zebra)—and he was right.

Rice and I made a détour and came to the edge of the wood within two hundred and fifty yards of the zebras. They were all hidden from me by a fringe of bushes—all except two. One was standing and one lying down. I fired, and a fat stallion fell where he stood. An instant later there was a great hammer of many hoofs, and the herd was gone.

We cut the dead stallion's throat and removed the tainting parts; then we covered him with branches to keep off the vultures, and followed up the herd. I was bent on killing as much food as possible while it was within touch, but try as we would the zebras always spotted us in the bush country before I could get in a shot. They are lazy animals, and it is not difficult to keep in touch with them by following the spoor ; but getting a shot, especially amongst trees, is quite another matter. Their glaring black and white stripes fade into the shadows and melt away amongst the lichened stones. You toil warily up a rocky slope, slipping silently from tree to tree, with rifle ready, eyes open, and head and shoulders bent; you keep one eye on the spoor, one eye straight ahead, and the third—the hunter's eye—rolling from right to left in case they have tried to outwit you by doubling. Then suddenly comes a warning snort, here and there the

outline of the ridge for one wild instant becomes a swinging head, a handbreadth of mane, or a moving croup; a
few rocks tremble and melt away; some shadows stagger
and, with a rustle of dead leaves and a clatter of hoofs,
the herd is gone. After a few hours of this sort of thing
we gave up the chase.

One of my commandeered carriers had gone on to
Mazimbagupa, and the women and men that he brought
back with him carried the meat to the kraal. While they
were skinning the zebra they lit a fire, and tasty bits of
the entrails they cut off and roasted on the coals. I traded
several sacks of meal and sweet potatoes and still had the
two hind quarters entire. The sacks were the native
article made of the bast of umsasas beaten on the trunk
and then peeled off. All this we took on to Urungwe.

We sighted Urungwe Kop about ten in the morning,
and at midday we arrived at Morrell's camp. A party of
Shangaan mine boys, building huts, as soon as they saw
us, jumped off the half-finished huts and ran down shouting 'Kazi feni! [1] ... Inkoos!' They seemed very pleased, and
took my rifle and the carriers' loads. The fly of a tent
was pitched in a small clearing, and in it lay Massikessi
Smith, reading a yellow-backed novel.

'Well,' I said, 'where is Mr. Morrell?'

'Hunting a green parrot,' said Smith; 'there used to
be two up here, but we had the other one for lunch
yesterday.'

'Why haven't you gone out too?' I asked.

'No use going out when there's nothing to shoot,'
said Mr. Smith.

---

[1] 'Kazi feni,' wife of an ape: 'kasi = umfasi,' wife; 'mab-
feni,' a baboon.

This seemed to me a poor answer, but I found out afterwards that Smith was gun-shy. I have known several dogs that were gun-shy, and most niggers close their eyes when they pull a trigger, but this was the only man I ever knew who was afraid to fire a gun.

James arrived about two o'clock, looking annoyed and disappointed; he had been chasing the green parrot from tree to tree without getting a shot. Smith had some steaks grilling on a gridiron and James cheered up when he had eaten one or two. James first of all gave a full ration of ufu to the boys (there were only about twenty in camp, for Paterson had started back for the wagons with the others) and then he had a good tuck-in. Neither he nor Smith asked what the meat was, and when they had eaten I told them it was zebra; they did not care a bit, but said that, zebra or not, it was very good. I was rather disappointed, because I had hidden all signs of the animal's identity, and thought they would shudder when I told them.

After a hearty meal they both went to sleep.

XI

GOLD-SEEKERS PAST AND PRESENT

During the Mombo-Monomotapa period these Makalanga, or 'People of the Sun', worked for gold and bartered it to the Arabs for copper . . . some of the Makalanga, while burying their dead in a sitting posture . . . laid beside them pots of poor material . . which once . . . held grain.[1]

I THOUGHT myself a great hero because I had relieved Urungwe Camp, but at fifteen one easily thinks oneself a hero. They had all been on short rations for some days and there remained only half a loaf of bread and half a sack of boys' skoff. So the Shangaans always spoke of me with admiration, James was impressed with my value, and even Massikessi Smith was moved—so much so that he confided to me that once, when landing in London after a long voyage, he had been arrested as Jack-the-Ripper. He also told me that his former nickname was 'Chimoio' Smith, earned by trapping an enormous number of leopards at the little rail-head village of that name. It had been changed to 'Massikessi' only through his having out-heroded at this border town his former herodism.

So I became a person of consequence in the camp; and James lent me one of his local natives to hunt with. Moreover, I told James of a kraal not far from Urungwe

[1] R. N. Hall and W. G. Nash, *Ancient Ruins of Rhodesia, 1904.*

where I had slept after leaving Mazimbagupa's, and advised him to send some of his Shangaans to tell the natives to bring in produce for sale; and this plan was very successful. Jack, the hunting boy, and I scoured the great plains and woody uplands round Urungwe, but beyond a few swimpey, or sand grouse, we got very little. But one day we came on a narrow vlei, six feet deep in long grass, and Jack, with an air of mystery, led me to a certain spot, and in an excited whisper told me that that was where his former baas was killed. His baas was a trader, and very keen on shooting. He had shot rhino, elephant, and buffalo, but he could not get a lion. One day some boys had seen a lion eating a dead water-buck, and they came in and told the baas. He hurried out and managed to get a shot, but only wounded the lion. They followed the blood spoor through the bush, until they came to this little vlei. Jack and the others implored him not to go into the long grass, but he was very keen. In he went, the lion stood up and faced him, and his rifle misfired. Then all the boys ran away, but after a while Jack and another boy stopped and went back. They cut great bundles of dead grass which they tied on poles and set alight. They frightened away the lion, and they carried the baas to the old Police Camp near Urungwe. But his right hand was chewed away, his stomach was torn, and he died.

I had been told this story in Sinoia, so I concluded that Jack was truthful. He took me to another place where vast stubby bones were scattered about, these were the bones of 'Nema', the rhinoceros that his baas had shot. He also showed me a wide vlei where the grass had been burnt, covered with hundreds of pairs of worm-eaten buffalo horns; but there were no bones here—the hyenas had seen to that. Great droves of buffalo used to graze on the rich vleis on either side of the Ruckomichi river, but they had all died of rinderpest four years before. Prior to that the young bulls used to amuse themselves by leaving the herd and chasing men and women who were travelling from one kraal to another, till they were forced to shin up the trees. Jack said that Urungwe before ' the sickness ' was teeming with game, and good shooting was to be had still, but later in the year; the game went down to the lower veld during winter.

James Morrell had come to Urungwe to open up what his Company considered was a new mining area. It was granite country, and as soon as I arrived I prophesied that he would never find any gold. He never told me if he found any or not, but I think that was his duty toward his Company; anyway, his mining operations were closed down in the course of nine months. Urungwe is a memorial of the labours of some forgotten race—and that is how, in a country where every hole in the ground is considered to be certain evidence of ancient gold mines, it had come to be pegged.

Along a low ridge running east and west there is a series of enormous holes. Besides this we found another hole some miles west, all being more or less in the same straight line. What they were made for, and who made them, I cannot even guess. One of them was big enough to have hidden a small church. James put in cuttings at right angles to the line of holes, and one day we heard a great commotion amongst the boys; they had come upon a skeleton. James and I spent all the morning in the cutting, carefully examining the bones. They were tightly packed in the earth, and quite soft with age. The skeleton was of a big man, facing the south. He was sitting upright, his arms hanging by his sides, and his chin resting on his knees. His skull had been broken in by a large stone, which still rested on top of it. Great quantities of broken pottery we found in all the cuttings, and many such skeletons.

When we had been about three weeks at Urungwe the wagons arrived; and soon afterwards a restlessness seized me, and I told James I was going on to look for the River. We always called the Zambesi ʽ the River ʼ. This meant that I should have to pass through the country labelled ʽ Elephants and Thick Bush ʼ.

James said he would come with me, as he wished to find out if food for his natives could be bought more cheaply in the valley. We set out one morning with perhaps a dozen carriers, with trading goods. When we had gone a few miles we came upon the main path from the north, and found two white men. One of them wore dark glasses, and a boy walked before him grasping the end of his stick to guide him, so we knew that he was blind.

We stepped aside from the path and bade him ʽ Good morning ʼ.

The man stopped and turned his face towards us. ʽ Good morning,ʼ he answered. Then he went on, ʽWill you have some tea with me ? Iʼm just about done. I canʼt see the confounded path and I keep on hurting my feet.ʼ

He laughed in a weak sort of way, and sat down. Two or three of his carriers came into sight, and then four *machela* boys bearing another white man in a rough *machela* made of sacks. The second man seemed in a worse plight than the first, for though the day was blazing hot he was dressed in thick clothes and a heavy overcoat and was wrapped in blankets; his mouth was half open, his teeth chattered like pebbles shaken in a boy's hands, and his tortured eyes, like an animal's, glared at us out of a sickly yellow face.

The *machela* boys plumped him down, and he essayed to rise, but could not until he was helped. Then he staggered over to his companion and lay down, pulling his blanket round him and letting his teeth chatter unrestrainedly. So long as we were with him he did not speak a word.

The blind man, however, after giving instructions to his boys to make tea, told us that the two of them had gone up to Zumbo by a route lying to the east of Urungwe. They had put all their trading goods into dug-out canoes, and had paddled up river with the idea of branching off up the Kafue to trade cattle in the country of the Mashakalumbwe. They had been overtaken by a sudden squall of wind, and all the canoes were capsized—the trading goods and rifles lay at the bottom of the Zambesi. Some of their boys were drowned, and others eaten by crocodiles, but they themselves and the larger part of their natives had swum ashore.

'But we have lost our money and we are ill,' he said; 'something has gone wrong with my eyes, and the other chap—well, you can see what he's like—the valley's not a health resort.'

We asked him if he had plenty of food, and he replied that he had. So we left him, and went on.

We camped that afternoon at a little stream whose banks were plentifully marked with the fresh spoor of lions. Indeed, lions seemed thick around Urungwe; but, though a couple of oxen were killed and the herd-boy treed, we never saw any.

Ill-luck was with me this trip, for I awoke next morning with a high temperature and a bad attack of malarial fever. There was nothing for it but to abandon our journey and return to Urungwe. A week elapsed before I was up and about, and my return to full diet was heralded by the arrival of Mr. Taberer, the Chief Native Commissioner.

He had been up to the Zambesi to investigate a case of murder and assault. It appeared that a certain half-breed Dutchman, recruiting labour along the River, had got drunk and shot the chief headman of a small village. The natives had then attacked and disarmed him, had seared rings round his wrists and ankles with burning faggots, and had tied him (bark rope round the scars) spread-eagle fashion to a huge baobab. They intended to leave him there to die of thirst. He was, however, rescued, and the searching arm of English justice was haling him, very much bandaged and emaciated, away to Salisbury.

Mr. Taberer told us that small-pox was sweeping through many of the kraals in the valley, and appeared to be travelling southwards. He warned us against going into Gandowa's kraal, in particular. He had gone as far as the escarpment with a Cape cart and six mules, and he told us that most of his harness had been eaten by hyenas; these brutes were so hungry and determined that they had time and again leaped into the cart at night, and had dragged out the harness, running off with loose bits even when they were chased and fired at.

As if to confirm this hyena yarn, it happened that the very next night one of my zebra hides disappeared. The thing was as dry and as hard as a board, and was pegged out on the ground to prevent shrinkage. We found the tracks of a hyena, and the displacement of dead leaves, grass, and bits of bark where he had dragged it through the bush. Of the hide itself we found no trace, and were forced to conclude that Tika had eaten it.

As soon as I was quite restored to health I started again for the Zambesi. James Morrell was prevented by a press of work from accompanying me. Rice went with me, and also two boys returning to Gandowa's kraal. The distance to the River, allowing for the very circuitous route, was about seventy miles. I expected to be away about ten days, and took as stores six pounds of flour, a tin of baking powder, six tins of jam, and a little salt. For meat and for Rice's food I relied on my rifle and a shot-gun that James lent me.

We purposed sleeping the first night at Gandowa's kraal—or rather, bearing Mr. Taberer's warning in mind, near the kraal.

At midday we overtook a party of eleven Mashaka-lumbwe returning from the Matabeleland mines. They were scattered on both sides of the path, chasing locusts. A small swarm had settled in the surrounding bush, and the men were chasing individual locusts and knocking them down with branches.

We marvelled that they found it worth while to spend so much time to so little purpose, for there is but little to eat on a solitary locust. In getting locusts for food the usual procedure is to collect the creatures at night, or at dawn, when they cannot fly, and are crowded together in tens of thousands on every tree. But the head-boy of the Mashakalumbwe pulled a long face and explained that the natives of the high-veld were unfriendly towards his tribe, and refused to sell them food. They were practically starving.

'So, baas', he said, laughing and rubbing his emaciated stomach, 'when we see a locust we chase it.'

A little later, when we stopped for lunch, Rice looked inquiringly at some majanji trees, remarking,

'Those men will find better food when they arrive here.'

He climbed one of the majanjis and brought down a billy full of large black caterpillars. We ate these with our lunch. I warn the reader against eating *any* sort of caterpillar; for all I know the ordinary ones may be poisonous. The table sort are not really common in Rhodesia; but when you find them they are always in large colonies. They are spiney and black, with whitish yellow rings at intervals, and are about three inches long. To prepare them: seize the caterpillar in the left hand; with the thumb of the right hand press in the animal's head, thus telescoping and disembowelling it; then cast the creature on the coals, and when it shrivels and the spines burn off eat hot—with the eyes closed. The flavour is distinctive and a little difficult to describe; a diet of these caterpillars has the disadvantage of leaving a slight burning sensation in the throat.

Before us lay a long stretch of dry country. At one point in it, beneath a clump of beautiful green vumbas, was a water-hole, but we found it dry. We pressed on a mile or two in the great heat, for we had got amongst the windless valleys and ridges of the escarpment, and the breeze failed us and the face of the high-veld, naked against the westering sun, was blistering hot. Then

I halted and waited for Rice to bring the water-bag.
Remembering the Sabi, I had brought a water-bag, and
I intended to keep its contents intact until I was very
thirsty indeed. Now I had become very thirsty indeed,
and I waited for Rice, intending to have one good drink
and distribute the rest amongst the three boys. But Rice
was unaccountably far behind. And when he came up I
saw his face, and knew and understood; and so I went
on still thirsting. . . . Poor, fat old Rice!

And then we came in sight of the valley—a vast,
sombre plain stretching ahead to the great mountains
beyond the Zambesi, and far flung to right and left.
Here and there amidst open country, or shouldering
aside the tangles of lesser growth, stood baobabs, their
vast boles, surmounted by leafless limbs, showing greyly
like the forms of monsters of the past. Over all the
valley lay a pall of smoke, blown up from some grass
fire, perhaps a hundred miles away.

I called a halt, and we all sat down on the path, each
where he was, and none of us looked at the other, for
we were all silent and ashamed, thinking of the empty
water-bag.

Suddenly I heard a slight exclamation, and looking up
I saw one of the Gandowa boys gazing at a little ridge
beyond the narrow gully that lay at our feet.

I followed his gaze, and, bringing my rifle gently to the
front, crouched behind a small boulder. Two hundred
yards away, and coming gradually into view like the hull
of a steamer on the skyline, was a sable bull. He advanced step by step, with his head down and his great
curved horns swinging easily to right and left, browsing
as he came. All the while he kept flicking one ear or

the other, and now and again he swung his horns back irritably to dislodge some particularly aggravating fly.

I glanced at the hammer of my Lee-Metford to make sure it was at full cock, and quietly raised the rifle. Two more heads appeared over the summit of the ridge; then two or three more. I waited. None of the boys made a sound. Then perhaps a dozen more heads appeared simultaneously, and thus by degrees a great troop of sable antelope, totally unconscious of the presence of man, came into sight.

I singled out the biggest bull and fired. He started sharply towards his left, walked about a dozen paces, and stopped. The other antelope put up their heads, looked round, sniffed, and went on browsing. I fired again. The big bull started forward a pace as if suddenly surprised, stopped, and then gently knelt upon his knees, put his shoulder to the earth, and lay down, lying motionless and half shrouded in the spare brown grass.

The rest of the troop appeared to take no interest in the matter. If they looked towards us, the sinking sun flashed wholly in their eyes, and evidently they could see nothing. If they sniffed the slight breeze that was springing up with evening, it brought them nothing but the scent of the baked earth and the smell of their own tracks that lay to windward of them.

Thinking of those starving Mashakalumbwe who chased locusts on the path behind us, I chose another bull and fired. He jerked up his head, gazing full into the sinking sun; then he stepped away a pace or two, and knelt down and lay still.

And even now the other sable appeared to take no notice. When the shot was fired they looked up and sniffed the breeze, and then resumed their browsing. It seemed to me incredible that they should be so totally unaware of danger. But evidently the sharp crash of the shots was something new in their experience. They could see nothing and smell nothing of danger, and because they were not stricken down they fancied themselves safe. Had we perhaps broken a twig, or rustled a leaf, or dislodged some tiny pebble, they might have realized the death that hung between them and the sun that flashed in their eyes.

A great bull that had hitherto been hidden by a clump of dwarfed umsasas stepped forward from his cover, browsing. And then temptation came on me—the sheer desire to kill— and I fired again. With a mighty snort he swung his horns against his ribs with a thump that boomed amongst the echoes of the shot and leaped away, sending the stones flying, and crashing madly through the undergrowth. For a mile we heard him snorting and tearing up the gully. Then for a little while was silence, and then a great gasping, and a bellowing of despair and death.

Not one of the troop moved. They stood like shadows among the long shadows of the trees. Not an ear turned. They knew now that terror lurked in the air they breathed. They knew not what innocent shrub, what harmless boulder, hid Death, the unknown and the terrible. Each remembered the lesson of his youth: to stand still until you *know*. Their old leaders, they who had brought them safely from the jaws of a hundred lions, were gone; and the new leaders of the troop, untried and inexperienced, blinded by the mocking sun and baffled by the scentless breeze, knew not.

Then I stood up. The sound of my rifle-butt against the ground, the scrape of my boots on the hard path, were slight sounds enough, but not lost on the ears of the wilderness. At last the young leaders knew. They gave the signal—how, I know not—and wholly together, like a squadron of cavalry on parade, the troop leaped to the gallop and crashed over the ridge.

It was night when we came to Gandowa. We camped outside the kraal. No one came out to welcome us, or to bring presents, for the hand of the plague was heavy on the people.

About eight o'clock the eleven Mashakalumbwe arrived. I bade them turn out the skoff-pots, and show me their catch of locusts. This they did, and we all (for the Gandowa boys were by no means anxious to leave me) laughed.

'Would you like meat,' I asked, 'so much meat that you cannot carry it?'

Then I sent them all off with Rice and the two Gandowa boys, to cut up and bring back as much of the two sable as they could carry. For myself I ate my supper, smoked a comfortable pipe, read a little by the firelight, and went to bed. About midnight the boys returned; their quiet, well-satisfied grunts thanking me more plainly than words. I called out to them that they might eat as much meat as they could. I awoke a little later to hear the Mashakalumbwe singing. They sang in a very low tone, very sweetly, for they had good voices and tuneful songs; nor did they cease singing till grey dawn was lighting up the foot-hills.

In the morning I went down to the water-hole where we got our supply. There was no other water within miles. Those sick of small-pox were lying untended around the hole, and when the thirst of the sickness came on them they crawled down, and dabbled their hands in the water and drank. Now the water-hole was but a small excavation in the bed of a dry river; at that season it never held more than five or six gallons; and those sick men and women, horrible to behold and still worse to smell, were drinking it, and washing their loathsome sores in it. This was the only occasion, through all my journeyings in Rhodesia, that I had my drinking-water boiled.

At Gandowa's kraal was a woman, lately bitten by a hyena. Just before the small-pox came there had been a great beer-drink, and after the dancing many of the people had been too drunk to crawl to their huts. They slept where they fell; and of these was the woman. Tika had seized her by the face, and had dragged her sixty or seventy yards before the cheeks and the flesh of the chin tore away, and she screamed. . . .

On that day we traded a great quantity of ufu, dried pumpkin, and sweet potatoes for sable meat; and I loaded the eleven Mashakalumbwe with this produce. I told Gandowa's people of the third sable, and bargained that in return for his meat they should have ready for me a certain number of loads of produce when I returned from the river. The people persuaded me to delay my departure for the next water-hole till evening, ' for ', they said, ' the path lies along the dry bed of the little river, which is white sand, very tiring, and, when the sun shines, as hot as fire.'

So it was about four o'clock that afternoon when we started out, and towards sunset we came to the dry-river path. We stepped into the white sand, and it sank under our feet like the sand of the sea-shore.

On either side of the dry river was an almost impenetrable thicket of thorns, fringed with green trees having a curious smell; and amidst this thicket rustled innumerable guinea-fowl, and unnumbered coveys of low-veld pheasants broke forth occasionally into their weird cries, which are like the creakings of ungreased wheels.

The place was alive with wild-fowl; on either hand the banks were pecked over and scratched into sand-baths, like the floor of a hen-run. Here and there in the dry river itself we came upon series of holes, perhaps thirty or forty in the series, and dug to a depth of about eighteen inches.

'What makes these holes?' I asked.

One of the boys laughed.

'Those are Machoko' (monkeys), he said. 'They dig in the sand for water. But one digs here and another digs there. They will not all dig together in one place, so they tire before they reach the water.'

Night came on us, and we plodded stolidly on, sinking deeply with every step. As the night advanced the sand cooled, and by degrees the air became chilly, and the curious smell of the green trees, which was rather like marigolds, seemed accentuated. The elusive sand was amazingly fatiguing; it sank loosely under one's feet, and as one stepped forward it slipped away behind. We were forced to walk nearly flat-footed. My thighs and hips ached with the unusual strain, and it was some time before I learnt to slacken down my usual pace to the pace of loose sand. I learnt afterwards that, if you are content to advance slowly, you can accustom yourself to the yielding surface.

After we had been walking a great while, as it seemed, I became very sleepy and tired, and found it difficult to keep my senses under control. Some of the boys walked in single file in front of me, and some behind. Suddenly I noticed one of the boys in front step out of the line, walk ten or a dozen paces to the right, start, sigh, and walk back into the line. A little while later another boy did the same thing. No one said anything: we were all too tired to speak. And as I trudged along presently a delicious sense of peace came over me; this endured a few blissful moments till I felt my knees giving beneath me. With what seemed an infinite struggle I tightened them, gasped, and started self-consciously to find myself ten yards from the line of carriers, and walking at a tangent from the path. Then I understood what was happening. We were dropping asleep as we walked, and as we slept we no longer walked straight, but staggered unconsciously from the track.

After many hours we came at last to the water-hole, and when we had drunk our fill, being too tired to fell a *scherm* or light a fire, each one of us lay down where he stood, and slept.

XII

THE ZAMBESI

Paths seemed to race beneath my feet;
I watched a duiker browsing stand
Among the guinea-fowl, while cool and sweet
Flowed blue Zambesi, close at hand.

On the following day we came at about three o'clock to the kraal of Dandawa, the paramount chief. The chief's own hut was the smallest in the village, but later in the day I noticed that all the women and young girls who passed this shabby little edifice stopped and curtsied before going on.

Very few of Dandawa's people had ever seen a white man. They scuttled off as we swung into the kraal, and the girls and women hid behind the huts and peered at us from under the eaves.

Dandawa was sent for, and he soon appeared from the neighbouring fields where he was working with some of his head-men. One of the latter spread the chief's mat under the indaba-tree, and Dandawa courteously invited me to sit on it, while he himself sat on the sand at a little distance, his head-men behind him.

We endeavoured to exchange a few compliments, but the dissimilarity of his dialect from anything that Rice or I knew made this difficult. However, fat old Rice put on his oiliest and most solemn expression, and for a good half-hour he and Dandawa murmured those gentle

and soothing phrases in use on polite occasions. I asked
Rice afterwards for a translation of Dandawa's welcome,
but the old hypocrite confessed that he had not understood a word of it. I rather fancy that there is a cere-
monial language for occasional use, which is complicated
and not generally known, and that the higher up you are
in the Bantu social scale the more complicated and high-
flown it becomes.

Most of the men of Dandawa's kraal appeared to be
absent from home. We reassured the women and girls by
a liberal gift of meat, and by degrees their fear wore off.
They arranged a dance in our honour that night.

The dance began soon after dark. Fires were lit and
thirty or forty girls and a few older women drew up in a
semicircle; I was invited to join the opposite semicircle
composed of the Mashakalumbwe, Rice, and a stray Dandawa boy or two. Some youths had brought out the big
tom-toms; these they hammered with surprising energy.
We struck up a chant:

'Whalila, whalila, kwam'tondoli,'
and we stamped our feet and clapped our hands to accen-
tuate the rhythm, at the same time bending our bodies
forward and swaying.

The girls were all nudging each other and laughing,
and carrying on a lively discussion that did not appear
to interfere with their singing. Apparently they were
urging one of their number to make the next move in
the dance, for presently, one of the girls, casting fear to
the winds, came dancing forward, hanging her head and
very shy, and selected me as a partner.

Not having the faintest idea of what was expected of
me, I was no less overcome by bashfulness; but fully

alive to my responsibilities as one of the governing race, I accompanied my partner to the middle of the arena, where I executed a series of uncouth steps with a frenzied notion of keeping some sort of time with the tune—a performance that even now brings a blush to my cheeks. My partner, with considerably more native grace, did the same. She then led me, still hopping fantastically, down the line of dancing girls who were consumed with ecstasies of giggling, until I selected one as my partner and my previous partner resumed her place in the semicircle. The Mashakalumbwe, as in duty bound, applauded vociferously; old Rice gasped speechlessly and shook with laughter like an enormous jelly, while the sweat of hilarity coursed down his ample figure; the girls themselves shrieked encouragingly and offered quantities of advice that I was wholly unable to take. My buxom young partner was naked to the loins, her hair was made up into little clay balls, her ankles clashed with palm-nuts; and I, emaciated with fever, pranced like an inspired stork. Sometimes in London drawing-rooms, or at Oxford balls, this picture has returned to me.

The whole affair gave every one concerned an immense amount of innocent satisfaction. The women asked me to be sure to spend a night there on our homeward way, and they promised to 'cook' stupendous quantities of Kafir beer with which to celebrate the occasion.

Old Dandawa the one-eyed (the other eye had been knocked out in a fight with the Matabele) seemed genuinely touched at our departure, and ordered a Chibanga boy to guide us on to the river. The Mashakalumbwe went no farther with us, their path lying to the west of ours.

Towards evening we came to Chibanga's kraal, and

were entertained with more dancing. The weather was very hot, and for the sake of the coolness we slept out in the open, near the path that went on to the river. When we awoke in the morning we found the tracks of a solitary bull elephant on the path, within a dozen paces of where we had slept. The old fellow had passed right through the kraal that night, not touching the grain-huts, which were as yet unthatched, not even rousing a dog. One of Chibanga's head-men offered to lead me to the solitary bull elephant before evening.

'There is a great pool over here which you can reach when the sun is so ———' (he indicated about fourteen miles by the sun). 'And there is another great pool over there, and that is where Indzoo has gone, which you can reach when the sun is so ———' (about ten miles). 'The elephants pass between one pool and the other. I will show you them.'

This offer I firmly declined. I noted the immense circumference of the footprint of Indzoo, I remembered many a torn and shattered tree, and I felt most unwilling to go a-tracking him. Had there been another white man —one whom I trusted—it would have been different; then the chances of being killed would have been reduced by half. Elephant hunters don't live long, anyway. No, no; should I meet Indzoo casually I should no doubt succumb to the temptation of trying him with one of those solid bullets that I kept by me; but I did not intend to go out of my way for an encounter.

Rice, the Chibanga boy and I then went on to find the river. The heat of the valley was very great, and no air stirred, so that at about eleven o'clock the Chibanga boy led us aside from the path to where there was water. The water lay in a low depression amidst a thicket of mapani. No grass grew around it, and the clay was trampled and scarred by the hoofs and pads of every creature of the wild. Here was the mighty print of Indzoo the elephant, there the round clean pugs of Shumba the lion, and Nya-rugwi the leopard. Coming down to the water in deep paths were the beaten highways of Nema the rhinoceros, for Nema always keeps to the same road. Here and there were tracks that might have been made by bear and cat; they were those of Tika the hyena and Impaka the wild cat. The strong, pointed spoor of duiker-buck and reed-buck mingled with the goat-like patterings of droves of impala, and over all lay the light three-toed markings of thousands of game birds.

Of water itself there was little. A few gallons of churned discoloured liquid, heavy with dropped feathers and rotting leaves and the excrement of multitudes of thirsty animals, was all that we found. To nicer stomachs the foetid smell of that water might have proved a deter-rent; but we drank it—three or four mouthfuls each (not more, for fear of dysentery)—and were glad.

At noon we came to the river. The path took us to a small kraal known as Inyamkai-iwa; a great baobab grew on the northern edge of it. 'Just beyond *there*', said the boy from Chibanga, 'lies the river.'

I passed on with a beating heart, and the next moment we saw the Zambesi. A mighty river it was, a thousand yards across, blue water dotted with white islands. Be-yond it, and quite near, towered a great range of moun-tains. But I had no eyes for the hills, I was all occupied with the river—there was such an immense quantity of water. The islands and banks were white sand, scarred with the tracks of hippopotami and crocodiles. I saw a flock of wild geese, some white ducks, and here and there a long-legged wading bird. Everywhere I noticed a slight smell of marigolds. Long, clumsy dug-outs were drawn up on the white sand of the watering-place; a shallow part had been chosen, where the crocodiles could not fling themselves on the women who came for water. The approach was an open sand-spit, naturally free of reeds, so that no crocodiles could hide and snap at passers-by.

We pushed off a dug-out and paddled into deep water, as I thought I should like a swim. Rice was terrified of the river, and crouched in the bottom of the dug-out. The boy from Chibanga, when he saw what I was going to do, was little better, because he thought we should capsize and he would be eaten by a crocodile. The people from Inyamkai-iwa's collected at the watering-place, and got very excited when I started swimming. Very few of them had seen a white man before, and a naked one at that. But no accident occurred, and the swim was delightful, though rather marred by the idea that something might rise up from the bottom and grab one.

After lunch we interviewed Inyamkai-iwa and arranged to have a couple of dug-outs ready on the morrow. I had expressed my intention of shooting hippo, and the chief said there were some large lagoons lower down the river where hippo were always to be seen. It was a wonderful place, he said.

Later on Rice and I wandered out amongst the trees. It was like a park—long glades of short brown grass beneath the massive boles of thorn and baobab. It looked as if the grass had been cut with a mower. We came upon a great herd of impala, looking like fallow-deer.

Early in the evening I became unaccountably sleepy and Rice spread my blankets in a half-finished hut. It had no roof yet, and I thought it would be cool. We lit a merry blaze and cooked some eggs and sweet potatoes. That evening I ate scarcely anything; I was so sleepy that after a few mouthfuls I lay down. As my head touched the dusty little roll of clothes that served as a pillow, a great regiment of mounted men came rushing towards me. I turned to Rice and asked him to help me, because I had fallen down on the sand and could not rise. Rice's face was grey with terror, but he caught me under the arms and dragged me along the sand just in time to miss the thundering hoofs. The horses were very big and richly caparisoned. The riders were in uniforms decorated with white strings and tassels, pennons streamed from their serried lances. They shouted as they passed us, but when they had gone past I could see them no more. The dust settled, and we saw huge buildings on the three sides of a square. We heard orders being given and from behind us poured in millions of cavalry. They thundered past us, shouting hoarsely. Thousands of marshalled lines dashed past, the lines twisted and wavered in the tumult, but the ranks never broke. The numbers were incredible—hundreds of millions of men; the cries deafened me; the excitement caught me by the heart and throat, and I sobbed and shouted and could not stop. But I seemed tied to the ground, I could not move, struggle as I would. A great dust went up but the flashing of swords and accoutrements showed through it all. The dust rose higher in the air, and the marshalled regiments drew away. Presently it became dark, and streaks of lightning showed

us that the dust had become rolling clouds. They rolled
and twisted with the wind, and the hosts of horsemen
galloped up into this, now showing plainly, now hidden
by the cloud-wrack. The shouts and cries grew dim and
dimmer, till they died down and were gone.

Then I found myself dreaming stories; they were the
most wonderful stories in the world. I lay quiet and
watched the stories grow. No human pen has ever attempted such tales. Each little one—they were so short
that I could see a dozen in every second—was as tremendous as the fall of Rome; their interest held me
spellbound; some of the stories had complicated plots,
and all through their marvellous intricacies *I saw them
happen with my own eyes*. Sometimes the tragedy of them
was so terrible that I found myself weeping aloud—they
took me right away into those places where there is no
hope. My heart hammered painfully with the excitement
of them, and often I could scarcely take my breath. Then
at last I came to a very gentle story ; it was most beautiful,
and wonderfully interesting. I longed to see what would
happen next, but the words and the figures of the people
grew slower and slower. I was so dead tired that I knew
I should fall asleep and never see the end. I struggled
to make my brain go on, but the people grew hazy; now
and again with an immense effort I saw them clearly, but
the words ceased altogether and the people all stopped
moving; and after a while they slipped into the dark.

When I awoke it was morning. The fire was burning
low, and the ash had accumulated to a great thickness;
this struck me as curious, because we do not burn big
fires on the hot low-veld. Rice sat by the fire, watching
me. His face was tired and anxious, and when I spoke to

him he at first did not reply. Then I stood up to dress, and told Rice we would see if the dug-outs had come. Rice rose at once.

'Baas,' he said, 'the dug-outs have been, and are now gone.'

For some little while I could not understand; then I asked, 'When did they come?'

'Three days ago,' said Rice, 'but the Baas was ill, and they returned down river.'

We stared at each other, and in a low voice Rice told me that for three nights the Baas had shouted and spoken wildly, and sometimes cried aloud; that he had not eaten nor was able to stand, so that Rice carried him when he asked to go outside. And Rice said that he was greatly afraid, for if the Baas had died the people of Inyamkai-iwa would have killed him also and taken the rifle and the shot-gun and blankets. 'Wherefore,' said Rice, 'let us go back to Urungwe, lest the sickness begin again.'

I thought over all this, and concluded that I had had a sunstroke when I swam in the river. So I called for the chief, Inyamkai-iwa, to bid him good-bye; he asked if three or four of his boys who wished to get work might accompany me to Salisbury, and when I had given permission, and they were ready, we left the kraal.

XIII

BACK TO UMTALI

'I wished to speak to these men, but the words were changed in my mouth, and all I could say was " Do not make that noise. It hurts my head ".'

RUDYARD KIPLING (*Rewards and Fairies*).

THE first night we slept at Chibanga's kraal; the next we camped at the water-hole half-way to Gandowa. Then we passed Gandowa's kraal where the people had been collecting baobab fruit for those sick with small-pox, of whom many were dead. We came to the rugged escarpments of the high-veld and left behind us the smell of marigolds. Palm and thorn and baobab we left below as we rose into the country of umsasa, majanji, and sugar-bush. The smooth alluvial paths and the shivering sand were replaced by jagged rocks that bruised our tired feet. The sweat trickled down from under my hat and dried before it reached my chin. The rising path skirted great kloofs and crested the razor chines of ridges. So we came to the wide horizons of the high-veld, seeing new sky-lines and dropping them again behind us, until we came to Urungwe Camp.

James Morrell had become nervous owing to my long absence, and had gone to the valley to meet me. He must have missed me when we were off the path, hunting, or he may have gone by way of Inyasikana's kraal. Inyasikana was a native chieftainess; her tribe always chose their ruler from amongst the young girls of a neighbouring kraal, and she was not allowed to marry; hence *Sikana*—the maiden.

I left a message for James, and, taking a few pounds of flour and half a dozen tins of jam, we went south. Soon a great lassitude seized me; every bone in my body ached; my tongue and lips grew dry, and even my eyes, so that I could hardly see. I stumbled along the narrow path catching my feet one over the other, assailed by a terrible weariness and irritation. I can still remember the shaking passion that caught at my throat when my hat blew off, and I had to stoop for it. The hot, dry hands of malaria were all about me, dragging me down. A fearful itchiness invaded every pore of my swollen skin. I would have given untold gold to be free to lie down and sleep; but I had to push on till we reached water, for without water my boys could not prepare their food.

Fortunately the high-veld was well supplied with little streams, so we had not many miles to go. I dropped down in the shade of an umsasa and fell asleep, and afterwards Rice spread my blankets and moved me on to them. Every alternate day for a hundred and ten miles the same thing happened: one day I was fit and vigorous, sometimes out-distancing my boys by two or three miles and chafing at their slowness; and the next morning the aching valley-fever would grip brain and heart and hand and send me staggering like a drunken man until we came to water. One day I would eat and shoot and talk with my boys, all eyes for the sweeping veld and radiant sky, and the next I would never touch food or speak, barely able to see the dizzy path under my feet.

We stayed the next day at the temporary kraal of Mazimbagupa, where lived the Matabele girl who was said to be bewitched. ' Mazimbagupa ' is a synonym for ' the generous ', like the name of the chieftainess Inyakwanikwa of Penhalonga. Other people called him ' Buk'aibenyo ', which may be rendered freely as ' the last of his family ', a title earned by his pleasant habit of clubbing, assegaing, or poisoning his near relatives.

The old chief came out to meet me. He was a tall man, a little wobbly on his large flat feet; rolls of loose skin hung about his chest and stomach, and two large unstable pouches had usurped his cheeks. His small eyes were set in a globe of wrinkles; he had no brows, eyelashes, or hair of any kind upon his face, and very little upon his head. But he was a nice old man and entertained us hospitably, drinking first a calabash-cup of each pot of beer that he presented to us, to show that it was not poisoned.

So I went on south, now sick, now well, till our salt and tobacco, among physical things the supreme solace of civilization, failed us. But the next day we crossed the Angwa, and in the evening came on the sunken wreck of Short's wagon. Very lonely it looked; the mud had engulfed one side even to the rails, and the long shadows ran out across broken yoke-keys and chain-lengths far over the empty vlei. Hardly had we left it, however, when we came on two cattle traders and a long line of carriers going north. The traders gave me salt and tobacco, and in spirit I blessed them, and went on.

The next day I spent as usual, groaning and half delirious, and on the next we fell in with the man who taught me the way of versification—Percy Erskine Driver, to whom I have never ceased to be grateful. Driver's own verses were humorous, sometimes imitations of Robert Burns, sometimes no higher than the limerick type. But he showed me something of rhyme and rhythm; and when, later, I attempted to put my own thoughts into words I learned to know and to appreciate the poetry of those greater than I.

Driver was a trooper in the British South African Police. He had been concerned in the Jameson Raid. At Doornkop he was struck on the head by a fragment of shell, and would have been disposed of by the burial fatigue, but for a timely recovery of consciousness. When I met him he was engaged on a dangerous medical mission to the kraals round about Imbowe's; his qualifications for the task consisted in the fact that he was quite without fear of contagion, and that he had spent some months studying medicine at Dublin (from which University he had, I gathered, been sent down). The small-pox had rapidly swept down from the Zambesi, and was killing great numbers of the uncleanly natives of the Lo Magundi high-veld. Driver had been told off to vaccinate.

I returned with him to Sinoia Police Camp, and was hospitably entertained by the Officers' Mess. They listened far into the night to my tales of the Bazizulu veld, and each of my stories brought forth another to cap it. But none of them had ever been through the wild bush-veld beyond Urungwe.

The next day I wanted to push on for Salisbury, but the Officer in Command told me with many regrets that he could not let my boys through until they had gone through a small-pox quarantine of, I think, sixteen days. I was furious, and told him that if I had known of his idiotic regulations I would have given Sinoia a wide berth and made for Salisbury across the open veld. He defended his position as well as he could, and as a concession said he would allow old Rice to go with me the next day, after he had been duly dipped in Jeyes' Fluid by way of a disinfectant.

With this I had to be content, and I resigned my scratch party of carriers to the Police quarantine, and my loads of skins and horns to the Officer in Command. The latter promised to send on the loads by the first wagon to Salisbury; but I never saw them again. As I afterwards found out, the man who had charge of the wagon bartered them for drink at the Royal Hotel in Salisbury.

A few days later Rice and I set out for Harare (Salisbury) by a short cut of sixty miles. Part of the second day I lay up in a native kraal with fever; but on the afternoon of the third we came within sight of outlying farms. I was feeling very ill and tired, but the excitement of getting back to civilization kept me struggling on. I suffered from a terrible thirst, for I was hot with fever, and the keen east wind which blew directly in our faces dried every particle of moisture from my lips. I had to call frequent halts, and when we halted I sat on my roll of blankets with my face towards Salisbury. Old Rice, seeing how exhausted I was, advised me to sit on the ground with my back against the blankets and my legs stretched straight before me. I tried this, and found the position far more restful.

We came in the dark to Salisbury, and I disfigured my face by stepping off a verandah and cutting my nose and

cheek against a piece of string that was hung out as
a clothes-line. I was too weary to enjoy the dinner to
which I had looked forward for some days, and my anti-
cipations of a long night's sleep on a spring mattress
came to nothing—I lay feverishly awake all night.

When morning came, however, and I had had my
bath, I felt very much refreshed; and, as a matter of
fact, since that time I have never suffered from a really
serious attack of malaria—nothing that lasted more than
ten days. I lunched with my cousin, the editor of the
principal newspaper,[1] and he plied me with questions
regarding the unknown district of Bazizulu. But there
was something unsympathetic in his manner which tied
my tongue; and when he finally remarked that a certain
young Smith (or Jones) would have got endless copy
from such a trip, I left him, and without resentment.
I did not in the least mind if people thought me stupid. I
had done something which they had not done, and I had
seen things which they had never seen, and I was content.

A few days later, when I arrived at Umtali, I found
that even my own people seemed little able to understand.
My mother, it is true, vowed that I was so thin that she
scarcely knew me; and my father said he would have
given ten pounds for my glimpse of Shumba the Terrible
—for he had never seen a lion; but I discovered that
what my eyes had seen and what my heart felt, my tongue
could never convey. Therefore I treasured my memories.
I saw James Morrell's strong face silhouetted against the
dark bush by the light of the fires; the shattering work

---

[1] *Now the 'Rhodesia Herald'. Under the title of 'The Mashonaland Herald' it was first brought out by Mr. E. W. Fairbridge as
a cyclostyle sheet, 27 June 1891, the first newspaper in Mashonaland.*

of Indzoo the elephant; the glossy skins of fat zebras as they stood dead-still in the chequered shadows; the black horns of Inyamkwarati among the broken stumps of burnt umsasa. As I sat down to the hearty meals of the frontier town the memory of the hungry Mashakalumbwe hunting locusts would flash before me; and I heard the shouts of *Kazi feni* when my party arrived with food at Urungwe. It all sank into my heart and fibre, so that to-day it remains with me as clearly as the paper lying upon my knee.

XIV

SIX MONTHS ON THE MAZOE

'In this Riuer we saw many Crocodils . . . some as bigge
as a boate . . . whose skinne is so hard that a sword will not
pierce it. His nature is euer when hee would haue his prey,
to cry and sobbe like a Christian body, to prouoke them to
come to him, and then he snatcheth at them.'

SIR JOHN HAWKINS (*Voyage . . . in 1564*).

FROM that time until the following May I sedulously
cultivated my eight acres of orchard and vegetable
garden. Old Masitembo had returned from Senna, bringing with him his nephew, Coffee. Coffee was bigger
and stronger than his uncle, but silent and very shy. He
and I became friends, and I admired his invariable
courtesy, his quiet manners, and capacity for hard work.
He, like other members of his family, played the malimbo,
the Kafir piano,[1] very well. But he was so shy that
I could never get him to play before me, although once,
when I was suffering from a bad headache, he played and
sang me to sleep.

Masitembo and Coffee entered my service and built
themselves a grass hut down in the garden. Masitembo
was getting old and his guile and vanity increased with
years. He was never satisfied unless he had several
changes of raiment, ornamental leather belts, looking-
glasses, a razor, and a score of other things of which he
caught sight when taking the vegetables to market.
Then he acquired a taste for curious tinned and bottled
foods. This caused Coffee considerable grief, for he

[1] *It consists of a wooden frame, with iron tongues of different
lengths fastened upon it in a row.*

wanted to save money and set up house when he returned
to Senna. Masitembo was not content unless Coffee
joined in his follies, and when his own money ran short
he never scrupled to borrow from his harassed nephew.

But Nemesis came one night. Masitembo had bought
a watch, and made Coffee do the same. Neither could
tell the time, but Masitembo constructed a sort of
bookshelf out of a condensed-milk case, in which he hung
the two watches side by side. He half filled the bookshelf with old magazines, over which he sometimes
pored—although he could not read—and on this particular occasion he set up two lighted candles on the bookshelf, so that he might know the time if he woke up in
the night. The result was that when the candles burned
down they set the bookshelf on fire; the flames spread to
the hut, and in a few moments watches, raiment, belts,
&c., had gone up in smoke—Masitembo and Coffee
barely escaping with their lives.

Masitembo was a splendid story-teller, and before the
hut was burned I used often to sit on my haunches in it,
listening to his folk-lore tales of Senna.

With the coming of dry weather in May, my father
and I went to the Lower Mazoe, in the district of
Maramba, where we worked six months. During the
whole of this time we never saw a white man.

I was sent on ahead from Salisbury by my father, and
told to make a camp on a certain part of the river which
I should locate from a sketch-map. The distance was, I
think, about eighty miles.

I camped two nights at the kraal of a chief named
Chignosha, about ten miles from the Mazoe, to see
a harvest dance on the following evening. In the morn-

ing came a tall youth from across the river, going back
to his home among the Mabudja. His hair was strung
with long lines of red beads, and he strutted about chatting
with the women who were preparing beer for the dance.
That evening, when I was tired of the dancing, and
had retired to my hut, old Chignosha came with me—
ostensibly to see to my welfare, but in truth to see a white
man undress. And the tall youth, Inyamkakudjga, presently entered; and when he had obtained permission, he
settled down with his hands towards the fire and recited
a piece of verse to us.

The poem told how, that morning, he and six other
men were returning from Fura to Matoko; how they
launched a dug-out on the Mazoe; how the demon who
dwells in the river had caught the dug-out in his arms and
sunk it; how Inyamkakudjga had been washed against an
overhanging tree; how the other six men had drowned.

It was the best example of extemporaneous verse I have
ever heard. The man never hesitated. He never gave
false weight to a gesture, but paused and spoke, halted
and continued, as if he had been learning the piece for
weeks. And yet the whole occurrence had only taken place
that morning!

The next morning Inyamkakudjga shaved off his crop
of hair and red beads in token of bereavement, and went
homewards; and my boys and I set out for the Mazoe.
I left the carriers and proceeded along the crest of a ridge
of hills to try and get a shot, taking a boy, Jack, to carry
my shot-gun. That little détour came near to costing me
my life. For as I walked carefully along the ridge I heard
a slight rustle in the grass around my feet. I stopped
and handed back my rifle to Jack, taking the shot-gun

from him; for I thought I had come on a covey of swim-pey. The rustling noise seemed all around me—now just behind, now in front; and I cocked the shot-gun and peered into the brown grass. Suddenly, without uttering a sound, Jack turned and bolted out of sight over the ridge. Something was amiss, and the next moment I had located that something. Around a hummock of brown grass, within a yard of my feet, moved slowly a slight strip of yellow colour. Without hesitation I levelled the gun, fired, and leaped for my life. A great threshing convulsed the grasses, and my hair stood on end. When this had died down I went forward, and found that I had shot away the head and neck of a big cobra. Those parts of him I never found, but with a steel tape-measure I measured what remained: and this was seven feet, six inches.

I pitched our camp and built a grass hut high up on the flank of a ridge overlooking a great pool. A week later my father came, and he thought that I should have chosen a better spot. We moved up river along the south bank, but found nothing better. So my father determined to cross over.

We constructed a raft of dry bamboos, and tied four paraffin cans upside down at the corners, and upon this Coffee and I essayed to cross. We took with us a long coil of bark rope which we intended to fix to the far bank as a ferry-rope. Half-way across a large stone stood out of the water; before we reached this our raft had sunk an inch or two below the surface, and by the time we got across, the hungry water of the Mazoe, which a few days before had choked the fellow-tribesmen of Inyamka-kudjga, was nearly to our knees.

However, when we had made fast our end of the ferry-rope, and the boys at the other end had pulled it taut, we had something upon which to lean our weight, and so made the return journey in safety. A day or two later I was passing the place, and noticed a curious increase in the bulk of the half-way stone. I looked again, and saw that a great crocodile lay basking upon its summit! I had seen crocodiles before, but this old fellow was a king of crocodiles. He lay flat and clingingly, his short arms and webbed feet clasping the rock beneath him. He was not red like the smaller crocodiles, but green; and I supposed this was due to a growth of aquatic weeds upon his iron hide.

I took my camera from its case and began to open it; but some instinct of being watched took hold upon him, and suddenly he stood up. I felt my hair tickle on the back of my head. I never knew that crocodiles could stand. I had always thought they merely floundered on their bellies. But, believe me, this crocodile stood up. I put down my camera hastily, and sent a bullet thudding into his massive flank, and with that he plunged into the water. We never saw him again; and whether he died of his wound or recovered I cannot say. But during the next six months I shot many crocodiles, and not one of them did I find dead; so I imagine the wounded are either eaten by their brethren, or they have a great power of recovery. I have shot them in the head, back, and flank; but always they dived, and were gone. Once I found one sleeping on a high rock; I sat down and plugged in a Lee-Metford bullet behind his forearm where I imagined his heart to be. He leaped—leaped out of his sodden sleep six feet into the air, straight for the eddying river, and I saw him no more.

The Masenna, who live by the Zambesi where crocodiles are a part of everyday life, have many stories of
Gnona. I have seen many men with scars upon their legs
—the work of Gnona. When they were seized they drew
the sheath-knife from their belts, and stooping under
water and feeling with their hands for the eye of Gnona,
plunged in the knife, and thus escaped. During the
February rains, they say, you may find full-grown crocodiles walking abroad on the paths. When Gnona is
hungry he will leap from the river upon a man as he
stoops to fill his calabash. When he is successful in hunting he pushes the victim into a hole in the bank, and waits
outside until the meat is gamey. There was a man at
Senna, named Butou, who was thus taken by a crocodile
and pushed into a hole in the bank. Butou was still alive,
and he found that the far end of the hole was free of
water. And as he lay there he heard the steps of men
and women overhead. And Butou worked terribly hard
with his hands at the soft earth above his head, and before
evening he came upon the dry bank, free and safe.

After all, when my father had explored both banks of
the Mazoe for a great distance, he decided that I had
chosen wisely ; and so after some days we returned to
the camp overlooking the pool.

Some months later my father was surveying along the
south bank and I upon the north. My boys were engaged
in cutting down bush, and as I had a free hour I thought
Vic and I would swim across, for I had not had a mouthful of English speech for a week or more, and upon the
other side I saw my father.

So Vic and I went down to the river where it flowed
very rapidly upon either side of a rocky island. And

because it flowed so swiftly I judged we were safe from crocodiles; otherwise I would not have ventured. We landed on the island and crossed a spit of washed sand. Then we swam the other part, and (with no clothes but a pair of boots and a hat) I joined my father in a cup of tea.

Soon after Vic and I made the return journey. And when we came to the spit of washed sand upon the upper side of the island, behold, the long dragging spoor and fresh footprints of a great crocodile overlying the spoor that we had made! For about ten minutes I sat on a worn stone and shivered. Vic understood the danger as well as I did, and she too shivered and smelt the fresh pugs. Deep water flowed on either side of us, and some-where in this water lurked Gnona—who might, even now, have his hungry reptile eye fixed upon us. I had neither knife nor rifle, and we were out of sight both of my father and my own boys. But something had to be done. As a preliminary I flung my boots on to the far bank. Then I collected a heap of big stones. Vixen barked furiously and I shouted at the top of my voice and hurled the stones into the water where we had to cross. Then with a final yell we plunged and swam for very life—never have I hated water so much!

No doubt if Gnona had been there on the spot, and hungry, these memoirs would never have been written. But evidently he was not, for we came safely to the bank.

At our Mazoe camp we never heard a lion roar, but lions sometimes passed through that country leaving the bones and hair of their kill lying in a trampled brake. One night Coffee and I were returning to the camp after a successful hour's shooting. We had seen a small herd of waterbuck down on the plain. Coffee and I set out after them, walking at high speed but with the habitual carefulness of men who depend largely upon silence for their food. We walked so quietly that presently I came face to face with a bushbuck ram. He was stepping lightly towards me, with his head in the air, nibbling delicately at some thorn leaves. But the sinking sun shone in his eyes, and the quiet evening breeze blew towards us, and even while he tossed his fluted horns in taking a leaf, he dropped suddenly with his spine broken. We pushed on at once, knowing that after hearing a shot game will often stand for a long while trying to locate its position. We came upon the open vlei, and stood for fully ten minutes without movement or sound. Then I stepped forward, and a dozen shades of grey detached themselves from the greyness of the open vlei and galloped towards the bush. The waterbuck were quite near. I picked out the bull, and brought him down, stumbling in the dust.

Coffee and I hastened back to camp, for he was one of those who are quite blind at night. Before we reached the foot of our camp-hill it was dark, and I had to walk slowly that Coffee might follow immediately in my tracks. Now and again he touched my back lightly with his out-stretched hand. And as we entered a thicket of bamboos I stopped suddenly.

‘ Do you hear that, Coffee ? ’ I said.

‘ Yes, Senhor, ’ he replied.

I moved on a few paces, and stopped again. This time the stealthy steps that followed beside us in the dark continued after we had stopped. Vic stood against my leg, quivering as though she were set on wires, and beginning the slow growl that I knew would end in a rush into the thicket. I picked her up, and gave her struggling to Coffee. She was one of those great hearts whose faithfulness knows no discretion.

We moved on again, and the light steps moved with us—one set a little in front of us, and one abreast. We were walking within almost arm's length of death. There was not much to hear, only the rustle of a pressed leaf now and again; but we both knew that this was Shumba the Terrible, the slayer of cattle and men. God alone knew what might precipitate the sudden leap.

I sent a low warning call into the darkness, ' He-e-eh! ' I warned—as I would a fractious cow. Both the lions hesitated : one's ears become keen under those circumstances; and I almost fancied I could hear the swish of the dubious tail.

' Shall I fire ? ' I asked Coffee.

' No, Senhor,' he said. ' We are carrying things in our hands; we have hats upon our heads, and clothes upon our bodies : it may be that Shumba is afraid. . . .'

The camp was not three hundred yards away, so we walked quietly on, though it was hard not to shout aloud for help; for we could hear the tinkling of the buckets and the laughter of the boys. And as we came nearer, the quiet steps ceased. And they rejoiced in camp because there was plenty of meat for the morrow; but Coffee and I were very quiet that night, and said nothing of what we had heard, until in the morning we took the whole camp down to see the footprints of Shumba the lion.

Of the Mazoe, although there is much to tell, I will say no more. Our hair grew long; our trousers grew short (for the thorns ripped away the legs bit by bit); and so did our tempers. We fished the river with dynamite, blasting the big pools and raising many a good

meal thereby. Food failed us on one occasion, and
I shot a she-monkey; my father ate some of it, but one
mouthful convinced me that I was not as hungry as
I thought. After some months we sent carriers to
Salisbury for provisions and newspapers. When the provisions came my father and I ate a pound of jam each; he
red currant, and I greengage. While we ate we read the
papers, and we learnt that the Boer War was over, and
that peace was declared. We read also that the 'King
was recovering, and the wound was healing satisfactorily';
from which we gathered that some dastardly attempt had
been made upon his life—for we knew nothing of appendi-
citis. We read also of the deaths of people that we knew;
and death seemed very intimate to us, out there on the
veld.

We used to snare guinea-fowl along the river bank,
and had good big game shooting. Waterbuck, bushbuck,
and koodoo were plentiful. Once I bagged a pheasant
and one of my boys with the same cartridge; but the
latter was more startled than hurt—anyhow, had he been
doing his work, he would not have been in the way.
We came upon the tracks of elephant, but never saw
Indzoo himself.

Sometimes we spent a few days washing gold in the
bed of the Mazoe; but on the whole we toiled steadily
and soberly at our vocations; my father surveying and
calculating, and I beaconing the property of the 'Susman
and Deary Alluvial Syndicate'. Umchena the White,
so called from the peculiar blackness of his skin, a song-
maker, made several new songs of unparalleled vulgarity in
honour of the Mazoe; Masitembo endeavoured vainly
to contract a *mésalliance* with several and various of the

buxom damsels of the neighbouring kraals; Coffee the
shy got a chance of putting something by for the new
hut in Senna Town, and one day, as an act of sheer
bravado, swam across the great pool, while I, expecting
every moment to see the swirl of Gnona, averted my
horrified eyes. . . .   When he landed, and stepped out
modestly beside me, his copper hide dripping with
water, I could have flung my arms round his neck. But,
'Coffee, you fool,' I said, 'there is only one Coffee.
Never do that again.'

Finally we packed up, and after six months' sojourn
in the wilderness we turned our faces homewards. And
on the second day my father was taken ill with dysentery.
Whereupon I doubled the loads, and made a *machela* of
sacks and a pole, and had my father carried for two days.
And when we came to a Dutchman's farm I abandoned half
the loads, for my father seemed very near to death, and
I had relays of sixteen boys to trot with the *machela*.
On that afternoon, between half-past one and half-past
eight, we covered thirty-two miles.   The tired load-
bearers streamed out behind us, only a few arriving in
camp that night.   One we lost altogether; his load lay
derelict by the roadside, but we never saw him again.
My father seemed better, and we stayed a few days with
a farmer.   Then again my father was smitten down.
Once he roused himself to say : 'Never mind if I die,
old Turnip-top, I shall be here with you in spirit.'

I hurried him on to the railway at Macheke, that he
might go from there to Umtali.   For myself I had to
stay behind.   For there were forty boys to pay, and no
money with which to pay them.   As my father left
Macheke I urged into his tired ear to have a wire sent

me to say that he was alive, and money to pay the boys. But both these things were swept out of his memory by the sickness and delirium. So I stayed on a weary week, not knowing if he were alive or dead. Every evening the forty boys came to me and demanded their pay. I would nod significantly at my rifle.

'The money will come,' I would say. 'Sleep you quietly to-night.'

But at the end of the week came the Dutchman with whom we had left the loads. Like a wise man he had been through the loads, making an inventory of all that was of value. And he had discovered certain heavy packets of gold and silver coin, and these he was bringing on to Macheke to send to us at Umtali; for he feared that his farm might be broken into. My father in his illness had evidently completely forgotten this store of money.

The Dutchman accused me bitterly of trying to entrap him—goodness knows what he thought of us! But I told him he was an ass, and took the money, and pushed on to Macheke. There I paid the boys, and Masitembo, Coffee, and I boarded a goods train for Umtali. Then the boys sang and danced beside the train, shouting out that 'Kamba', as they called me, would return to Mazoe; and they chanted the songs of Umchena, the song-maker, and called after us asking if we remembered the kill at the lower camp, or the great beer-drink at the main camp, and other things of a like nature. But whether this was mere excitement at seeing their first train, or because they were relieved to get their pay, or because they had all enjoyed life on the Mazoe, I cannot say.

XV

INTROSPECTION AND A RESOLVE

> Great joyous heart!
> Lone lover of the unkempt hills! . . .
> Hoarder of things heroic, whose far eyes
> After strange dreams still farther strain and pass . . .
> Who on Death's road—by all the flowerless ways he went—
> Hath raised great gates of triumph, crowned above
> With calm conviction, underbuilt with love . . .
> Take, ere the songs be done,
> This song from me, thy son.
>
> *(Chikwira Makoma.)*

I WAS sixteen when we went to the Mazoe; there I learnt to know and love my father. Although there were times when we did not meet for days, yet dangers faced and difficulties overcome together brought us very near. Looking back now I see him as a very young and light-hearted man, with a happy nature which not even the struggle for a livelihood and the great hardships of the early days could overcloud. To the natives he was *Chikwira Makoma*—climber of hills. Yet in spite of the deep sense of comradeship which existed between us, there were things which I never told him.

I was not happy—no, I was not happy. I suppose that the hard life and my frequent illnesses had given a sombre turn to my thoughts. While my boys slept I used to sit for hours on my blankets, tending my little fire, while Vic cuddled beside me. Above us the umsasa leaves trembled and shook with the hot air from the fire;

beyond them the blue of the heavens was silvered with the stars. Those nights the heaviness of spirit, which had assailed me now and then, came down on me like a cloud, and plunged me into a gloom which was without belief and without hope. At times, of course, the cloud lifted, and I forgot everything but my scheme for bringing farmers out to Rhodesia. I could tell no one about it as yet, the beginning of it was hidden from me, and the end lay aeons ahead. It was not merely one man's work, like the painting of a picture ; it meant the result of innumerable forces and dreams—like the working of a good farm. It was my Vision Splendid.

I had another dream at times. It was of a firelit room —dark except for the firelight. Outside were pine-trees and drifting snow, which emphasized the comfort within. Before the fire lay a girl with an open book in front of her. I could not see her face, although I felt that some day I should see it. I was by her side, and we read the book together. I poured out all my thoughts to her ; she understood, and we were very happy.

Meanwhile I felt that I must work. The harder I worked and the more I knew, the nearer I should be to both visions. When I returned from the Mazoe I was seized with a great desire to visit England ; also I wished to go back and see my friends at Grahamstown. There is no time like the present, I said to myself. So I went round to the Bank, drew out my balance, and went home to pack.

First, however, I offered the roll of money to my mother, and said that I should like her to go down to the Cape for a change—a change that no one ever more greatly needed or had more richly earned. But my

mother was very sad, and said that she would never
return to the Cape, but charged me with many messages
to her mother.

So I packed my two portmanteaus (they became mine
by the simple process of commandeering them from my
mother's stores) with the queer bits of clothing that made
up my wardrobe. There was a silk tennis shirt that my
mother had given me one Christmas ; and there was
my peaked felt hat, along the rim of which was scored
my kill of big game in the Mazoe trip ; and there were
various things which I had darned and patched with great
care beside strange camp fires.

Our journey was a long one, some eighteen or nineteen
hundred miles. We were delayed in Bulawayo three days,
but beyond this we travelled pretty continuously, and on
the evening of, I think, the sixth day, we arrived in
country that I knew of old, the Karroo around Kim-
berley.

For many hundred of miles past, the sight of burnt
farmsteads and deserted blockhouses, sometimes well
punctured with bullets, and those little open scantzes—
where the snipers had lain for many a weary day—riveted
my attention. It was the country that I knew and understood ; had it not given birth to me, and to my father,
and to his father before him ? It was a land of brave men,
of bitter battles. The dust of these winding roads, strewn
with boulders, had stirred beneath the tread of the fighting men of England. Over these vasty plains, silent and
scarred with sun, had swept the bullets of the Five Nations
of the Empire. Boer and Briton, each had shed his blood
amongst the sparse karroo-bush and the crimson aloes.
These things came into my heart, and I longed to see

some way whereby Boer and Briton might, now, after they had fought their inevitable fight, pull wisely and wholly together to free themselves of the black cancer that ate at their vitals, weakening, dividing, threatening. White men of frugal habits and strong physique—yes, South Africa needs not tens, but tens of thousands such.

And so at length we came to Grahamstown, where every kopje, every kloof and Kafir boom, and little isolated untidy patch of prickly-pear, recalled memories of my childhood. It was but six years since I had left Grahamstown, but in that time how much had happened!

Arrived in Grahamstown I suddenly found myself in the midst of my former girl playmates and school friends, now grown into a careless, pleasure-loving crowd of flappers and college men. And I was mightily surprised to find myself enjoying not only a considerable popularity, but a whirl of gaiety—picnics, music, boating, fishing, dinner-parties—I felt like an out-at-elbows man-about-town who has unexpectedly come into a fortune! Moreover, I had a pocketful of money, and small financial limitations which galled and cramped my old school-mates only brought me into wider request.

After a time, however, I suddenly tired of the careless life at Grahamstown. I bade farewell to my friends, booked my passage for England, and, three days later, I stepped on board the *Kinfauns Castle* at Port Elizabeth.

XVI

ENGLAND

All of a sudden his heart and will
Cried out to God for a wild bird's wings
To fly from the snares and the cruelties
Out to the veld, where men are few,
Where Peace is rous'd by each sunrise new,
And God leans down from His lonely skies!
ARTHUR SHEARLY CRIPPS (*A Way Out*).

I SET foot in England for the first time in March, 1903.
The first thing that I remarked was the apparent nearness
of the grey sky. In quick succession I was surprised by
the youthful look of the people, by the fresh damp smell,
by the dirtiness of the walls of the houses, by the vivid
green of the fields, and last—but by no means least—by
curious stripes that lay across many of the meadows. It
was not till years later that I discovered that these stripes
were caused by rolling the grass in spring.

As we drove along the narrow, winding streets of
London, a sense of keen disappointment came over me.
I had expected a city of gold and white, mighty thorough-
fares, imposing edifices, solemnity. Instead straggled
long lines of grimy three-storied living-houses, ill-lit and
uninviting. Instead of stately processions of dignified
citizens, conscious of the responsibilities of Empire, I
found throngs of smallish, active, young-looking people,
shouting, running hither and thither, vending papers and
posies and penny toys. Cartoons and advertisements
flared at me from every hoarding.

This was Saturday evening; I had only about seventeen shillings in my pocket, and my grandmother had told me she was moving, so I set about waiting as cheaply as I could until I got her address from her Bank on Monday. I got my bed and breakfast for, I think, 5*s.*; for lunch I ate nothing, and I converted dinner into a fairly light afternoon meal which consisted of a cup of cocoa, 2*d.*, and a bun, 1*d.*

My amusements had to be cheap also. Two or three of us went down the Strand to Piccadilly that Saturday night, and I was accosted by a benevolent old gentleman who presumed that I belonged to the Wild West show at Olympia. I had never heard either of this entertainment or of Olympia; and I was highly indignant that an Englishman could not recognize a fellow Englishman when he saw him. But this incident called my attention to my sun-bleached peaked hat, upon the rim of which was scored my big game kill on the Mazoe. I determined to get a bowler.

I awoke the next morning to a tremendous silence reigning over the City of London, a silence broken only by the twittering of numbers of sparrows down in Charterhouse Square. As soon as I had had breakfast I hurried outside to see London. The sparrows appealed to me tremendously; every breath of the damp air seemed fraught with new things. . . . I peered through the iron railings at old Charterhouse School; I found an old friend, a very grimy fig-tree, growing against a wall in the Square. Then I went forth into Aldersgate Street and discovered St. Paul's. I knew it was really St. Paul's because a policeman told me. I did not go inside, not because I did not want to see the inside, but solely because I did not want to go 'to church' that morning. Then I found Watling Street; and immediately felt more at home, for the Watling Street is mentioned in *Hereward the Wake*. I felt towards Watling Street rather as the other Colonial felt towards the 'bus-conductor whom he recognized from the day before—his only 'friend' in London.

The following morning, Monday, was a revelation to me. Instead of my empty Aldersgate Street and my deserted Cheapside, I found the City throbbing with life. Great tides of people swept the pavements, the roads were invisible for the throngs of drays and cabs and 'buses. I made my way, from policeman to policeman, to Clement's Lane. But it was not until the following afternoon that I got my grandmother's address. She had taken a flat in Victoria Street, and invited me thither with all speed. To my grandmother, the frail, wise, and valiant, I owe more than I can say; and all the time I was in England her house was more than a home to me.

I love England. She cured me of a bitter sickness, of bitter hatreds, of bitter ignorance. The English summer filled my ears with song, and my heart with gladness. The grey keen winter rested eyes that were over-tired with gazing against the sun, and healed nerves that were frayed and ragged. In the quiet cold of autumn, in the dark rains of winter, in the boisterous keenness of spring, I discovered a plodding energy of which I had never dreamed. I love England for her surpassing history, and I love her for her youth. But I saw sights there which, had they been told me, I should have thought incredible.

One Saturday evening I walked from Trinity Mission in Stratford to Whitechapel. As I left the doors of the

Mission two women began an altercation. The elder of the two had evidently been drinking. In a moment they were fighting—a spectacle that to a man acquainted only with 'savages' was infinitely repulsive. A big, kindly-faced policeman hurried up and separated them, pushing aside the children who had gathered round, and taking the elder woman into her house.

Not far off a bully was knocking his wife about. The negroid races are not supposed to hold women in respect, but such an incident as this I have never seen in Africa. Yet English women subscribe money to send missionaries to the blacks, while their own sisters are treated thus! Should we not put our own house in order first?

In a vast community like Great Britain thousands of children are born every year who, by the death of one—or perhaps both—of their parents, are left homeless and destitute. We leave these little orphans in the work-house, we do not give them a chance. We do not give education a chance—wide, far-seeing education *by* the educated, based on handicrafts and land culture.

I was never weary of exploring London streets, travelling on unfamiliar 'buses, and watching the people. I was fond of dropping in at out-of-the-way eating-houses, for there I had opportunities of meeting many strange people. After the purchase of a bowler hat I was never taken for anything but a Londoner. Now and again while 'taking a glass' with some friendly carter or publican I divulged the fact of my South African birth, and this never failed to elicit surprise. I was, on these occasions, invariably complimented on my correct English; and I never escaped a certain inward bitterness when the fact that I was *white* was commented on.

Soon after my arrival I went down to Welwyn, in Hertfordshire, for the day. And there, for the first time, I saw a daisy. I went down on my hands and knees on the wet turf to see it closer, and when I looked up I saw that all the field before me was carpeted with daisies. I rose and went forward among them as it were upon wings. This was the land of my fathers, and now—the more that all my life I had been defrauded of it—it was my land. Pride of race, love of the land, unfolded that day within my heart.

I visited Leeds, Norwich, and Edinburgh, and made the inevitable comparisons between the great over-crowded cities and the lack of population in South Africa. Again and again I resolved to get farmers and farm-labourers for Rhodesia. Yet it began to be borne in on me that long training would be needed to fit clerk or casual labourer, or even farm hand, for the constant calls upon the initiative, patience, and knowledge required for agriculture in Rhodesia. Farming is supposed to be easy. Yet by the side of agriculture medicine is child's play. A farmer should know biology, chemistry, botany, and bacteriology. Geology and meteorology will be necessary to him; a sound working knowledge of engineering and carpentry will be among his best assets. Every successful farmer must have a knowledge of markets, finance, food values, horse-management, butchering, dairying, and so on. Eight years' schooling would barely give a man a glimpse of the possibilities which lie before a farmer. Nevertheless, I intended to succeed in my scheme ; and I spent many a long hour thinking things over, until the time came for me to return to Rhodesia.

XVII

I RETURN TO UMTALI

Long since from Beira Bay I sailed.
Low coast-line, sands, and sea
(That eve of eves I sail'd forlorn)
Alike wore grey for me.

This morn of morns I came again,
'Tis eve in Beira Bay :
What overspills of Ophir gold
Have flooded out the grey !

ARTHUR SHEARLY CRIPPS (*Beira Bay*).

I JOINED the Deutsch Ost-Africa Linie's S.S. *General* at Rotterdam in November ; it was from the same boat that my mother and I landed at Beira in 1896. For the first eight days the Purser, a German passenger and I were the only persons to take meals in the second saloon. They were for the most part cold collations of sausages and tinned fruit that one had to get down as best as one could. All day and all night for eight days we steamed into the very eye of the wind, while the seas crashed over the forecastle head and flooded the barren well-deck, sweeping away the lifebuoys and even tearing away part of the taffrail from the upper deck. The noise was never-ceasing, the galley rattled with pots and crockery, the engine-room hissed with splashing water and groaned with straining timber, the rigging screamed against the wind, and the monstrous ' thud ' of the seas ahead was always followed by cataracts of water rushing off the forecastle, and alternated with the ' blob-blob-

blob' of the skied propeller. I have always looked back upon that eight days' storm with considerable pleasure, and was proud to think that our craft was British built. The battling, the fight against the sheer blind hate of Nature, had in it a touch of the heroic that appealed to me.

A few days later we put in at the port of Tangier. Some months previously I had written to the Kaid Sir Harry Maclean volunteering my services in the campaign that was being carried on against some pretender to the Moroccan throne. The Kaid's secretary had replied saying that I had no chance of being enrolled in the army of his Shereefial Highness, as the sacking of Europeans from the army was the order of the day. The civil strife was still in progress, and that night, as we lay at anchor, we could hear from time to time an outburst of firing. But for some unknown dignitary's dislike of Europeans I might at that moment have been touring the desert on a camel, and trying to support on its tottering foundations the unsteady throne of Morocco.

At Beira I fell in with an old friend of mine who took me round the town till about one o'clock next morning. 'Round the town' meant 'round the pubs.', where, for the most part, I drank ginger ale. Returning to my hotel, I found I had for room-mate an old gun-runner and illicit spirit distiller of Central Africa. He was extremely drunk, and was trying to get into his pink flannelette nightshirt, which he had carefully laid out on the floor, by crawling into it. He told me that whisky-manufacture was the simplest thing possible. A healthy crop of bamboos, a few large native pots, a disused gun-barrel, and a wet sack were all that was necessary for the distillation of an admirably intoxicating spirit. He looked as if he had been trying some. During my stay in England I had been sure that there was no place like Rhodesia, no life like the frontier life. Now I began to have a little twinge of doubt. There were, after all, other ways of living.

I arrived back in Umtali after an absence of twelve months. My people were fit and well, but times were bad. The long low roof of 'Utopia' gleamed amongst the grenadillas as of old. The lines of red geraniums and fruit trees on the terraces in front of the houses were thriving. Everything was pleasantly familiar. But one face was missing, the scarred, anxious face of Vic— little Vic who for nine years had been my faithful friend and inseparable companion. She had been taken by a leopard only a few weeks earlier. Fearless and true, she was not one to feign sleep (as many a dog will) when the fierce veld robber was about; she had gone forth in a last endeavour, and died. I cherish her memory, and no one has ever taken her place.

XVIII

THE NATIVE LABOUR BUREAU AND OTHER MATTERS

> Dusty with travel they return,
> And silent with long journeying.
> In spring,
> When the first thunderstorms are in the air
> And the hot roadways burn,
> Up the Main Street they come,
> Bandawi, Tshangaan, Senna ;
> The labourers, going home.
>
> *Veld Verse.*

THE first few weeks after I returned home I carried on my gardening and helped my father. Then one day came a note from Mr. Horace Freeman, asking me to call on him. Mr. Freeman was a mining and general agent, proprietor of the *Rhodesia Advertiser*, and secretary to various bodies. I had known him for years. He told me that he had been appointed agent of the Rhodesia Native Labour Bureau, and wanted some one who could speak the native languages. He offered me ten pounds a month if I would take this on and help him with his other work.

Times were bad in Rhodesia, and I could not afford to refuse the billet. I have ever since been glad that I accepted it. Mr. Freeman was a good master and a man I enjoyed working for. He never spared me, but he worked twice as hard himself. I kept the *Advertiser* books and collected the accounts—the latter task calling for tact, humour, and a certain amount of courage.

My duties were legion. On one occasion, I remember, I had to repeg a claim, battery and all, the 'Discovery Notice' of which had inadvertently been allowed to lapse by the owner, one of the public men of the country. I did this under the very noses of the two men who were managing the battery. On another occasion I repegged the chief claims of the old Bodlonfa property at dawn, in the teeth of several other parties who were on the same quest.

The Labour Bureau work occupied a fair part of each week. We had a force of native recruiters in uniform, and the boys we recruited we sent on to the Wankie coalfield and the Rand mines. We sent off as many as 130 in a party. This work was always interesting, and gave me an insight into the characters of all manner of natives, from the skilled hammer-boy of Matshanga to the merry untrained fellows from Senna, and the malcontent 'Christians' from Bandawi.

The head boy of our native recruiters was one Sjambok, a son of the chief Katerere by a slave woman. He was as fierce and ill-tempered a little man as I have ever met, and it was his way to show scant respect to all but a favoured few. On one occasion Mr. Maritz, the friend and hero of my boyhood, came into the office to pay a bill. Sjambok, who was measuring out some rations of meal, stood suddenly to attention, stiff as a ramrod, exclaiming in a tense deep voice the salute of the fighting tribes:

'Inkoos!'

'Huh,' retorted the taciturn South African, and presently Sjambok left the room.

'You know Sjambok?' I said.

Maritz settled his six foot six slowly and with impressive deliberation into my typing chair. He held up his long brown hand and extended his index finger towards the blue horizon and the barren rocks of Murawha's hill that lay beyond the township.

'I have known Sjambok seventeen years,' he grunted. 'He was the same then as now, no older, no younger. His mother was a slave, his father a king—a fierce man. Sjambok was my slave then—when I was king . . .'

He paused, and his lean finger tapped meditatively towards the skyline.

'Katerere gave him to me. There were no white men then—no houses—no roads' (he slowly spread his hand and with a little movement brushed aside the civilization of which we white men boast)—'I was there alone. There were no others.

'Then Heyman came. They forestalled Andrade and Gouveia at Umtassa's, they cheated the King of Portugal of country that did not honestly belong to him, and Bernard O'Hara—you remember him—took Andrade and the Baron Rezende as prisoners to Salisbury. Colquhoun was Administrator. The Company got Manicaland and blamed Colquhoun for getting it.'

He laughed noiselessly.

'Heyman consulted me. I told him where Massikessi lay. We went down to the low-veld, we fired six rounds with the seven-pounder—we only had seven rounds in all —and then we charged. . . .

'The Portuguese cleared out on the other side. We

hoisted the Union Jack. We took candles and potatoes and boots. One man commandeered the Government gold-balance. Oh, we captured a great slice of territory that day, and we got stores enough to provision our new gold-belt on the Umtali.

'Then Heyman went back, and he took the Portuguese guns for Fort Hill at the Imbeza Junction—where the first Umtali was built. He left me as Administrator of the Manica low-veld.

'Me and Sjambok, just the two of us, alone in Massikessi, and, by God, we administered the country *well*! All the niggers came in. There were hundreds of wrongs to be righted; the Portuguese could not understand the people. But I understood them. The people came from Penga and Venga and Vumba; they came in hundreds from the low-veld and beyond Vumba.

'And I will tell you: I kept the *records of my administration* . . . I wrote it all down in the books we had taken from the Portuguese. I used their green ink, and I blotted the writing with their red sand. The Portuguese did not use blotting-paper, they used red sand.

'I sat on the verandah in front of the Court-house. The English flag waved on the Portuguese flag-post in the Court-house Square. The people squatted in hundreds in the Square, and I righted their wrongs and wrote down the record. Sjambok stood beside me, and I kept my saddled horse hitched to a verandah post—for I did not know when the Portuguese would come back.

'And so at last the Portuguese came back. It was breakfast time, and the people had not come into the Square. The Portuguese were lining the wall by the main gate, and they fired into the Square—the bullets hopped in the dust like locusts, like very quick *voet-gangers*.

'I cut down the English flag, I carried it in my hand, and I jumped on the horse.

'There was only one way out—a little gate. Sjambok would have liked to go first. He did not like the bullets that hopped like *voetgangers*.'

The big man sitting on my typing chair turned suddenly towards me, snarling and baring his short teeth that gleamed like a lion's above his grizzled beard.

'But in those days I, too, wanted to live. "Sjambok, you dog," I said, "keep behind me; you will keep the little bullets off the horse's legs!"'

He laughed, and waved his long forefinger at the hills beyond Murawha.

'And my horse stuck in the little gate!'

'Sjambok was hopping and skipping behind in a way that made me laugh. "Inkoos," he shouted, "Ow! the little bullets . . ."'

'Then my horse got through, and in a few minutes we were safe. I am not fond of writing, I never keep accounts; I have never kept them; I will never keep them.'

His face hardened.

'But I had kept the Records of my Administration— *and I had forgotten them.*

'Oh yes, I know Sjambok. We are old friends. He was then as he is now, no younger, no older.'

He rose slowly to his great height. 'Receipt? Thank you.' He walked out of the office. Sjambok, on the verandah, stood as rigidly to attention as a soldier waiting to be shot.

'Inkoos!'

Maritz did not even look at him.

Ten pounds a month did not allow me the luxury of taking meals at the hotel, so I used to take a few jam sandwiches to the office every day. Mr. Freeman would be away fifty or fifty-five minutes for lunch; my lunch took perhaps ten minutes; so there was always a little time over. I employed this in trying to write verse. I sent off a couple of pieces called 'The Sniper' and 'Closed Down' to the editor of the *South African Magazine*, and to my amazement they were not only accepted at a guinea each, but the editor complimented me on them. When Mr. Freeman arrived back from lunch that day I showed him the letter.

'You see', I said, 'I make more money in the luncheon hour than all the day put together.'

'What cheek!' said my master, laughing; and I could see that he was tremendously pleased.

I worked for Horace Freeman for two years and a half. This was my period of 'town life'. Many things happened. I am not proud of them all.

I paid a flying visit to the Shangaan Chiefs in Gazaland, covering two hundred and seventy miles in thirteen days. I had a strange encounter with a troop of baboons near the 'Grand' reef. I played cricket for Umtali—being tenth man or thereabouts—and polished up my tennis. I paid short visits to several parts of Rhodesia that I had not before visited. I was one of the founders of the Progressive Club. I wrote occasional articles for the 'Buster', as Freeman's paper was nicknamed, and interviewed a number of prominent South Africans on their way through; I translated also several folk-lore stories from the oral Chisenna, some of which afterwards appeared in

Mr. Andrew Lang's *Orange Fairy Book*. I got a certain amount of shooting with the young men of my acquaintance, and was considered something of an authority, having a little more veld-craft than most of them.

I was harassed by an inexplicable restlessness, and goaded by an energy for which I could find no outlet. I slept very badly—sometimes not for three nights together. My cure was always the same: on the fourth night I would take my blankets and wander away into the veld to lie down among the long grasses. There is no kinder ceiling than the sky ; no finer philosopher than the darkling night.

XIX

A REMINDER AND INGWI

Far, far away the brooding mountains lie,
The silver streams that croon among the ferns,
The wide umsasas black against the sky,
The dreaming valleys where the glow-worm burns.
The veld has vanished with the closing door—
The veld that shall be Ingwi's never more.

Veld Verse.

I HAD been trying to collect some money from one of the ' *Buster's* ' debtors. My bicycle had punctured, and I was wheeling it. It was one of those fiercely hot days in summer, when one closes one's eyes against the glare that beats off the road and the iron houses; and as I walked I ruminated.

When you close your eyes on a hot day you may see things that have remained half hidden at the back of your brain. That day I saw a street in the east end of London. It was a street crowded with children—dirty children, yet lovable, exhausted with the heat. No decent air, not enough food. The waste of it all! Children's lives wasting while the Empire cried aloud for men. There were workhouses full, orphanages full—and no farmers.

' Farmers—children, farmers—children . . .': the words ran in my head as I pushed my bicycle along the dusty road.

And then I saw it quite clearly : *Train the children to*

be farmers! Not in England. Teach them their farming in the land where they will farm. Give them gentle men and women for their mentors and guides, and give them a farm of their own where they may grow up among the gentle farm animals, proud of the former, understanding the latter. Shift the orphanages of Britain north, south, east, and west to the shores of Greater Britain, where farmers and farmers' wives are *wanted*, and where no man with strong arms and a willing heart would ever want for his daily bread.

I saw great Colleges of Agriculture (not workhouses) springing up in every man-hungry corner of the Empire. I saw little children shedding the bondage of bitter circumstances, and stretching their legs and minds amid the thousand interests of the farm. I saw waste turned to providence, the waste of unneeded humanity converted to the husbandry of unpeopled acres.

'This is a Great Thing,' I thought; 'I must think it over. I must be cautious. It is all so plain—so simple. I may be mistaken on some points. But if I am right, I will put this thing before the people of England—so help me God!'

I had been given a message, and the great difficulties began to present themselves. There were moments of bitter lucidity, when for a moment the curtains were drawn aside and I viewed the path that lay ahead. Always I shrank back, sick and appalled, and fear sat in my soul and gripped upon my heart like a live thing. Always I comforted myself, thinking of the children who would be happier, of the bare acres that would bloom.

A leopard took to following me at night; sometimes I took this as an evil omen, and at others as a lesson to teach me to be brave. I would hear his quiet footsteps sometimes on the path behind me, sometimes in the long grass beside me. His footfalls were as light as feathers, but he could not hide the stealthy 'grind' of the loose sand, nor the parting of the brown grass before his muzzle, nor (but this was at great intervals) the sudden 'crish' of a dried leaf that he had overlooked. These almost soundless sounds were never lost upon me. I have no unusual physical attributes but one, and that is the faculty of being able to distinguish between the sounds of the veld. The veld is very quiet at night, the silence strikes people of noisier lands as terrific. By day, of course, it is never quiet for a moment: one can always hear birds and lizards and insects moving; and even at noon, when animals are asleep and there is no breeze, one can hear the unceasing rustle of growing or wither-ing grass, the warping of grass-seeds and dead wood in the hot sun, the splintering of tiny atoms of rock, owing to unequal expansion, and often the loud 'popping' of umsasa and other leguminous seed-pods. At night the veld is quieter, but I have often lain awake listening to the white ants working near by, to little insects, attracted by the light, that squeeze and push their way towards the camp-fire, to night-birds eating the ripe fruit in some dis-tant fig-tree. I have often heard, too, the various sounds made by game when they scent or see the fire, the sudden halt, the whistle of Bhima the reedbuck, the snort of Inyamkwarati the sable; other sounds, too, and more significant, like the single grunt of Shumba the lion, or the triple 'Huh-huh-huh' of Ingwi the leopard. The dullest ears can hear the fierce grunts of Shumba, and Ingwi, and Tika—for some reason or other they mean you to hear them; but other animals rely greatly on their quietness. Yet I have got many a meal by hearing sounds at which my boys, though they wore no noisy boots and had been bred in the veld, had not even guessed.

Slowly I worked out a scheme for emigrating orphan and destitute children to South Africa. The scheme ran always in my head as I pursued my daily task with Horace Freeman, and ever at night when I walked home, sometimes at a late hour, to 'Utopia'. And for four months Ingwi the leopard kept me company at night, gliding stealthily amongst the long grasses and the wild custard-apples. Once I saw—or thought I saw—him, on the path just behind me; I heard the 'grind' of the loose sand under his feet, and I turned very quickly to see his lithe shadow leap silently out of sight. He was perhaps six yards from me, perhaps less.

Of the emigration scheme I said nothing, but I told my family about Ingwi. They all laughed at me. Even my father laughed, so I said no more.

Then I took a Mauser rifle with me at night, and Ingwi wisely absented himself. Then I left the rifle at home, and Ingwi came back again, a little bolder, I thought, than before. Again and again I felt that if I did not stop and face him, Ingwi would leap upon me. I used to pick up a goodish lump of stone (I knew all the stones along the track) and turn upon the vague shadows of sound where Ingwi lurked, and call on him quietly by name.

'Ingwi, Ingwi,' I used to say, 'come along now while I am ready for you, Ingwi!'

I was insured for a little sum of money which was to come to me at twenty-one, a matter of about two hundred and thirty pounds with the bonuses. I had saved a little more. With this capital I hoped to get to England. I intended also to go by New Zealand and Canada, to see these countries and determine if there were any chance of the scheme operating there also. By staying with friends in New Zealand and Canada, and by travelling second- or third-class, I estimated that the trip would cost only about one hundred and sixty pounds, including all expenses. Now a cousin suggested that I should try to get a Rhodes Scholarship; that was a matter of three years at Oxford, with three hundred pounds a year for expenses. I saw the possibilities of the Scholarship idea, and wrote immediately to the Rhodesian Director of Education. The latter replied that if I qualified for Oxford by passing Responsions he was prepared to recommend me to the Rhodes Trustees.

About that time I was surprised one night to find a neighbour's dog in a very excited condition on our verandah. Next morning no one in the house could account for the animal's presence, till our neighbour himself arrived and said that when returning from ' Utopia ' to his house on the previous evening, a leopard had struck at the dog from the long grass. The dog had narrowly escaped, and fled incontinently back to our house.

My father looked at me a trifle apologetically.

Seven days later Ewan Tulloch stopped me in the street to tell me that a friend of his, a contractor working on the Melsetter Road a few miles out of Umtali, had been attacked in broad daylight by a leopard, had grappled with the brute and stabbed it to death with his sheath-knife, and was now lying, dying of his wounds, in hospital. He died that night.

' Ingwi,' I thought, ' O Ingwi, you who killed my

little Vic; now you are going out of your way to find trouble.'

Not many days after this we awoke one morning to find our hen-run robbed, and on the wire netting under which the robber had burrowed his way clung two or three of the hairs of Yellow Eyes. Fifteen or sixteen fowls had been killed and taken; there were none left in the run.

Then I set a trap, calling in the aid of my father. We summoned up all our knowledge of the veld. We borrowed a fierce-looking leopard trap, with blunt and savage jaws—things that would not cut, but would hold, hold like the grip of death. We baited the trap—with nothing! We just stood it on the floor of the hen-run, and covered it with a few handfuls of sand and grass. Over the great gin we hung two tempting hens, suspended from the beams in an open-work cage.

'It is enough,' said my father, 'Ingwi will stand up to reach the hens; they are a trifle high for him. He will move forward his hind foot to get the extra reach, and that hind foot will touch the spring.'

At one o'clock I was roused by a slight noise and knew that Ingwi was caught. I took a lantern and my rifle and stepped lightly to the door. The doorway was hidden from the fowl-run by a corner of the house, so Ingwi could not see me; he thought himself alone. I heard him turn restlessly from side to side of the run. I heard curious, plaintive sounds, like the weeping of some lost little animal seeking blindly for its mother. The little wistful cries came to me out of the silence of the night, so questioningly, so brimming with fear, and yet some tiny hope, that, for an instant, my heart was flooded with pity. I turned sick at the thought that I had brought this thing to pass. Ingwi had come upon a tragedy such as it is given to few to know. Ingwi, the incarnation of subtlety and cunning, whose life was spent in laying traps for others; Ingwi, the very breath of freedom, pulsing with life, supple and puissant, was outdone, trapped, held fast for all to see. The pillars of his universe had collapsed about him. Yet still in those cries was a faint note of agonizing hope.

I stepped out beyond the corner of the house. There was a crash. *Ingwi was not trapped.* The trap lay sprung on the floor of the run, the cage containing the hens lay in the hole under the wire netting. He was free, but his freedom was bounded by four walls and a roof of ter-rible wire that sagged and gave and shook under his rushes, but would not break.

There was no cry from Ingwi now, but like a streak of light he leaped from one side to the other, tearing at the wire with claws and teeth, reaching up and dragging at the roof, flashing his fierce lambent eyes at me, his ears back, tail lashing, trapped—trapped—trapped!

I waited until Ingwi was at his finest, stretched half across the run, his head straining against the wire, his teeth buried in a roof-beam, a low furious snarl choking in his throat. Then I fired. And the body of Ingwi slid to the ground, harmless as a dewdrop, soft as a kitten playing in the sun.

XX

GOOD-BYE

What are the roads I seek for now?
Hungry like those I know so well?
(The hard sun bit on eyes and brow)
Now who can tell—now who can tell!

The dust lay thick on blade and leaf,
The dust lay hot on rock and road,
It was all dry as parting grief
That is not said or showed.

I WORKED up to two days before my departure. Then Mr. Freeman paid me and further wrote me out a cheque for ten pounds as a bonus. He also offered me a partnership in his business when I returned from England.

The next day I set out in the direction of Old Umtali to find my father and bid him good-bye. I found him on the road beyond Christmas Pass.

I said, 'Good-bye, Dad; I am going to England.'

He said, 'Why are you going? What is behind the Rhodes Scholarship?'

I loved my father, but I hated laying bare the dream of my boyhood. But I had known that he would ask me, and I meant to tell him. My heart beat heavily, so I waited a little, just as one waits before shooting, after a long and tiring stalk.

Then I said, 'I am going to England to try and get farmers here. I want to get poor children from the orphanages and the towns, and I want to train them here.'

My father looked steadily at me. 'How will you do it?' he said.

'I don't know yet,' I answered; 'but England is rich; there are many rich people there. Perhaps I will find some who will provide the money. . . . It will benefit England, it will help the colonies, so I think people will see.'

My father understood at once, and I was very glad to see him look pleased.

'But it will be a hard job,' he said; 'you will not find the right people at first. It will take you two or three years.'

'I've got some money,' I said, 'and I'm trying for the Scholarship. If I get that it means three years in England.'

'Yes, yes,' he said, 'I think they'll give it to you—if you can pass the exams. But you will come back to us soon?'

He looked round at the great sun-baked hills with a little gesture.

'I don't know how long I'll be,' I answered, 'perhaps only two years. Perhaps it will take me all my life.'

My father's face turned suddenly very serious.

After a while he spoke again, very quietly, and with a little laugh. 'These people,' he said, 'all these people you are working for, they may never know what you have done, they may never thank you.'

I remembered my dark hours. 'I know,' I said.

We were both silent awhile. Then my father asked me why I was going to New Zealand and Canada, and

I said, ' To see if there is room there also for child immigration,' and he told me to see Earl Grey when I was in
Canada, and to ask his advice.

We did not say much more, but my father told me
again to come back soon. We looked at each other for
a little while; and then my father took my hand and
kissed me, and turned away.

When I had gone some distance I stopped and looked
back. It was blazing hot, the dry road quivered under the
sun, and the dry red dust lay deep. My father was standing in the middle of the road, looking after me. His
grey flannel trousers to the knee were red with dust, for
he had come some miles to meet me. He wore a soft
felt hat, very battered, and carried a cheap white sunshade.
He usually carried the sunshade in hot weather, and had
often asked me to use one too, but I preferred my rifle.
We waved our hands, and I went on; and that was the
last time I saw him.

So I went back to Umtali over Christmas Pass. From
the summit of the Pass I could see north over the Gold
Belt to Umtassa and the mountains of Inyanga. To the
south the great heights of Vumba and Dora were deeply
blue in the afternoon light, and the shadows stretched
out behind the granite peaks of the Odzi country. East
and west towered Inyamutshiri, while far away below me
straggled the little township of Umtali in its cheap brick
and corrugated iron.

I went down the Pass home, and packed my two portmanteaus. And the next evening I said good-bye to my
mother and, with the two boys who carried my kit, I
walked down Main Street to the station.

At Cape Town I exchanged the luxury of the Zambesi

express for the sordid overcrowding of an emigrant ship bound for New Zealand.

On the 30th of August I landed at Vancouver; from thence I went to Nelson on Lake Arrowhead, where I was granted an interview by Lord Grey. I had hoped for ten minutes of his time, just to set my scheme of child immigration before him. Instead, we talked of it for just one hour, and his comprehension and sympathy are still vividly before me.

Winnipeg, Chicago, New York—I saw them all. At last I sailed by the *Etruria* for Liverpool.

XXI

'SMALLS'

The hours are passing slow,
I hear their weary tread
Clang from the tower, and go
Back to their kinsfolk dead.
Sleep! death's twin brother dread!
Why dost thou scorn me so?
       ANDREW LANG (*Ballade of Sleep*).

I WAS glad to get back to England. The cold fresh smell of clay made me feel that I should be strong enough to do my work. The first step was to pass 'Smalls'. The name suggests something inconsiderable; it comforts me to think that it was too much for the defender of Mafeking, and twice laid low the stalwart Gladstone. The truth must out; 'Smalls' shook me to my very foundations —or lack of them. Gladstone's failure I multiplied by two; but in extenuation I plead the fact that I had left school at eleven, and for ten years I had been a stranger to study.

After my third failure my old enemy insomnia returned. And here there was no kind brown veld to which I could take my old blankets, and on whose breast I could lie content, watching the wheeling stars and resting in the silence. Here in Oxford there were bells—bells everywhere, shattering the night; and taunting imps laughing in my ears with prophecies of yet another failure.

On going up to coach in Oxford I threw aside every

thought and interest that was not 'Smalls'. I began work at nine, at one I stopped reluctantly. At two I began again and went on to half-past four. From half-past five until a quarter-past seven I laboured on, then changed into evening-dress for dinner at 7.30. Dinner took an hour and a half, for old Mr. Penny, my coach, dined after a gracious, old-fashioned style. After dinner I would write lists of Greek and Latin words or idioms till eleven, and then tumble wearily into bed.

Ten hours a day of manual work is good for a man ; but ten hours of grinding study leaves one's brain in the position of a cat with a brick tied to her neck. Very often I never put my nose outside the house all day.

I was trying to cram into eight weeks the work of the ordinary schoolboy's eight years. As a matter of fact the passing of 'Smalls' cost me in all ten months' study.

Towards the approach of the second examination Mr. Penny grew nervous, and asked me what I should do if I chanced to fail.

'I can't afford another attempt,' I said.

'No, my dear fellow,' he replied, 'don't say that. If you fail, I want you to take a five-weeks' "easy" and come straight back to me. You will give me the greatest pleasure if you will allow me to have you as my guest next term. If you pass, you can repay me, little by little. If you fail, you must think no more about it.'

I tried to pretend that it scarcely mattered to me whether I satisfied the examiners or not, but he would not listen, and insisted ; so at length I promised. Later, I was glad enough.

Very soon the reward of perseverance became patent ; old Mr. Penny was delighted.

'But don't overdo it, Fairbridge,' he would say; 'don't over-train, my dear fellow.'

It seemed that all went well, though in truth I was too dazed with the eternal effort, too surfeited with my mental orgy, to be conscious of well or ill.

The week before the examination began I spent in a daily and nightly contest with toothache. Three abscesses at the roots of three molars, and the final extraction of those reluctant molars themselves, sent me into Schools as shattered and miserable as the most perverse imp of misfortune could desire. However, when the papers appeared before me I found them very much to my liking, and the delight of fluency amid all that tricky folly quickly banished all memory of the dentist. Mr. Penny and my mathematical coach were in the highest spirits.

On the afternoon of Friday remained only the paper on geometry, a subject that I considered simple. Certainly this particular paper seemed easy enough. I went quickly through the first half, but at the next question some little hitch occurred. I saw how the problem worked out, but somehow could not just do it. I tried it two or three ways, and then I thought I had found it. I worked it out—to an absurdity. I had reached the water-hole, to find it filled with sand!

I took a deep breath and marched on. My next stage was equally barren. I left it and pushed on to the last. And then a strange thing happened: from somewhere behind the desk at which I sat stole an invisible hand, soft but irresistibly firm. It moved quietly along my neck and pressed gently against the back of my head. My head sank a little with the weight, and I shook it suddenly and irritably.

There we sat in the great bleak wing of the New Schools, around us the grey gloom and the pacing vigilators. Between the high, cold walls the evening fog of Oxford City lay level athwart the windows and the stone. Yet all I saw was a long strip of white and flaming sand where the fierce sun flickered along the million ripples of a great river, with crocodiles basking sombrely at the water's edge! Again and again I stooped to work; again and again that cunning hand stole quietly along my neck and pressed irresistibly upon my head. I sat upright, and the weight was gone; I stooped, and it returned. I propped my papers before me and tried again. But it seemed now that I was not sitting upright but stooping forward; and the weight of that terrible hand pressed my face down and down towards the paper.

I sat at my desk fighting the old sunstroke and the examiners until five o'clock, and then I returned to Banbury Road cursing the day I was born.

Nevertheless old Mr. Penny did not take a gloomy view.

'The paper must have been exceptionally difficult', he said (he knew nothing of mathematics), 'or you would have been able to master it. In that case they will lower the standard.'

I went home to my grandmother at East Grinstead. On Monday morning I received a letter from an official of the Rhodes Trust saying that he had been into the Schools on Saturday and was happy to see that I had passed.

I have said that I went home to my grandmother. Not only my grandmother lived at East Grinstead. There is something of which I should like to write and yet I may not—and indeed could not even if I might. Only this can I say: I had been in that firelit room which haunted me out on the veld; I had been within it not once but many times since January snow had given place to spring. One morning I shall never forget. After a question asked and answered I carried my happiness out into the winds. The beeches at Balcombe were coming into leaf. In among the green leaves flashed the sunlight —golden-green among the bronze and emerald. The wind and the colour and the music were beautiful as hope. . . . When the ecstasy had quietened I found I was in a lane. There were men trimming the hedges—quiet men who did not look at me. Other men were plough-ing, others were ditching, others again followed the fur-rows sowing seed. I seemed to see a very host of shadows —men of the land who had worked and loved. I took off my hat to them—I who was alive and loved.

You will understand now that it was not only my own people who were glad with me when that telegram came. It was not they and I alone who were hurt when another telegram came which read: ' Afraid there has been some mistake. You have not passed " Smalls ".'

I think then that I should have given up—not given up the scheme of Child Emigration, for that had become part of my life; but given up all thought of Oxford. But my grandmother was of another mind.

' Try once more,' she said.

But it had become a case of trying to try. My brain seemed like a worn-down ploughshare that will no longer grip. There was no more strength in me. Physically and mentally I went to pieces. The memory of that time still hurts.

Such is the irony of things that although I had not worked half an hour a day for the past seven weeks, yet, when I sat for 'Smalls' in June, I could find nothing in the papers that seemed anything but ridiculously simple and familiar. I was always among the first to finish each paper, and I remember wondering whether it was not all a gigantic mistake. But mistake or not, I did not care. I answered the questions unhesitatingly, threw my paper into the box, and strolled out of the Schools pulling out cigarette and matches.

'Plough away!' I used to mutter.

When it was all over I was packed off to the Shetlands —I had not even energy enough to arrange my own holiday. Standing outside the little store which is the telegraph office at Hillswick I read the telegram from Mr. Penny assuring me that there was no mistake this time—I really *had* passed.

On the former occasion the official of the Rhodes Trust had walked into the Schools, seen a list of men entered for the examination in Responsions with my name upon it, mistaken it for a list of successful candidates, and written his congratulations.

I turned with success still warm upon me and looked out over the rounded head of Rona's Hill, down the long arm of sea called Hamer's Voe, over which the salt sea-wind came sweeping, and wondered what the next step in my life would be.

The answer came in due time to me : a Rhodes Scholarship and Exeter College.

XXII

OXFORD

The fighting man shall from the sun
Take warmth, and life from the glowing earth;
Speed with the light-foot winds to run,
And with the trees to newer birth;
And find, when fighting shall be done,
Great rest, and fulness after dearth.

JULIAN GRENFELL (Into Battle).

VERY clear in my mind still is the sensation of arriving at Oxford. Dicky Spread, a former fellow-pupil at Mr. Penny's, met me, and we drove out into the October fogginess together.

'What are you going to do?' said Dicky, 'I'm going in for boxing.'

'Well,' I replied, 'I had thought about Law . . .'

'Oh, *that*! You had better take up Forestry with me. They say it's the easiest school going.'

Poor Dicky, he believed it. I had not known that anything so human could be studied at the University, and welcomed the suggestion. As for boxing—

'A fellow has got to *do* something up here,' remarked Richard.

Quite so; and if one *did* something for Oxford one could at least claim a hearing. I quickly revised my ideas, and made up my mind.

My father had once told me that every Englishman

should know how to box. Here was my chance, and I did not mean to let it slip.

'Foot work first, sir,' old Barry used to say. Short-cuts to fame jarred on his sense of thoroughness. By slow degrees he revealed to me the use of hit and jab and hook and counter.

I entered heart and soul into the game, studying Tommy Burns and Gunner Moir, and trying to turn their science into art. I discovered for myself, by great good luck, the trick of the heavy punch, and found it of great use. When the Novices' Competition approached at the end of term a fit of enthusiasm seized me, and I volunteered to fill a gap in the Middleweight section. It was really rather a silly thing to do, especially as I had been laid up some days with malaria.

'You'll be orl right, sir,' said Barry, trying to be cheerful, 'just keep a straight left, and step back.'

The night of the competition came, and I saw Dicky Spread win his event. Personally, I knew I had not the slightest chance, but I wanted to distinguish myself by making up in spirit what I lacked in ability. My opponent was Julian Grenfell, of Balliol, a man I had often sparred with in the instruction ring. He was a little heavier than I, and of the same height, with some previous experience of the ring, and a free-hitting style that made him a pretty boxer to watch, and an ugly one to face. Grenfell, I think, was very keen to win his Blue, and had literally 'been all over me' so often in our friendly spars that he had no reason to doubt the result. It was, in fact, a foregone conclusion: I lost.

To be a 'Blue' or a 'Half Blue' is greatly desired by most 'Varsity men; with many undergraduates it is a more telling distinction than an Honours degree. I felt sure that if I could win my Blue in the ring I should have laid the foundation for much good work.

I went back to East Grinstead in high hopes. A score or more of Exeter College men who had never before spoken to me had readily broken the ice by starting conversations with a reference to my first competition. Men of other Colleges seemed glad enough to recognize me when I met them casually. In fact to the end of my three years at the University I kept on meeting men who said they had seen me box against Grenfell. The *'Varsity* said ' No one who was present will forget the rounds between Grenfell and Fairbridge'. All this was so much to the good.

I knew that I should win my Blue; in my heart I had no doubt of it. But to win it I had to train and practise and read. . . . I lost no time. I had a punching-bag erected in the miniature rifle range at East Grinstead, and here I regularly repaired, hammering away for half an hour with an old pair of gloves that I had picked up second-hand. I skipped and danced and did Müller with unswerving perseverance. Every day at 12.15 I sallied forth for a run along the country roads, where most of the natives stared after me as if I were an eccentric ourang-outang. But some of the old sports among them would cheer me on.

So I returned to Oxford at the beginning of Hilary Term very fit and well, though rather light in weight, and set about learning all I could of Dave Barry's art and ring-craft.

I spent at least four afternoons a week at the gym, and the other three I employed in long country walks, interspersed with sprints between telegraph posts. But for one whole week, just before the Prelims., my nose was so battered with continuous heavy sparring, and my thumbs and fingers so swollen and knocked about, that I had to abandon boxing and make Barry wrestle with me instead. He would lean up against me, and try to ' smother' me, while I closed with him and jolted him with my arms and shoulders, as in in-fighting.

During this time I formed a friendship with a man who was to play a considerable part in the launching of Child Emigration: Frank Day, of New Brunswick and Christ Church, a candidate for Heavy Weight honours; a grand fellow, a colossus of size and strength, weighing some fourteen stone.

' Just sitting in the sun is what I like,' he used to say.

The night of the Prelims. came finding Grenfell up to weight and me at ten stone thirteen, that is, giving away six or seven pounds. Nevertheless, I had no qualms about the fight. As we stood together before a blazing fire in the dressing room he said:

' This is the worst moment of my life.'

I strolled from the dressing room into the hall and watched the fighting. Dicky Spread was knocked out by a Keble man—poor old Dicky, he was over-anxious. Corker of Trinity was knocked out. Bunco Brown of Worcester was practically knocked out—the fight was stopped, I think. Pearson and Townsend was another stopped fight—Fenwick and Bosman's another. Frank Day knocked out Basden—right through the ropes into the stalls. Yes, it was a night of knock-outs and hard hitting; a good augury for my right cross-counter!

Then Grenfell went out and stepped into the ring. There was a volley of applause. He was a fine-looking fellow, tall and straight and lithe, and when stripped not unlike that bronze Hermes who sits looking out to the right with his cap on his head, his wings on his feet, and his caduceus in his hand.

I stepped in after him and went over to old Gee, my second, in the far corner. There was to be no excitement, no mixing it up this time, *before the third round*, and I looked quietly round the hall. Here and there was a friendly face, nodding encouragement: poor old Dicky who had been knocked out, Cameron of Balliol, a lusty squad of Exeter men, and Otho Shaw and Edmund Burke from Mr. Penny's. It is a curious sensation, sitting in the ring just before a scrap, where one man is pitting his heart and brain and sinew against yours. He hopes to call up all that is good in him, all that is cunning, all that is strong, to the end that he may defeat you—and win his Blue. It is a time when you wish you had led a better life: fewer cigarettes, less wine, no gorging, more healthy exercise. I have seen common pugilists, nearly beaten, upon whose faces shone this virtuous desire so strongly that the blood and the blueness and the beer showed no longer and only simple heroism remained.

Gull stood up to introduce us.

'Mr. Grenfell of Balliol—Mr. Fairbridge of Exeter! Seconds out of the ring. Time!'

Grenfell opened restrainedly, but he soon had one to my face and a heavy one to my stomach. That woke him up, and to my delight he slipped immediately into his free-hitting, left-lead, chin-in-the-air style. I tried him tentatively with a cross-counter. It effected nothing, and it did not scare him. I tried him twice more in the same round, without result.

We went to our corners with Grenfell well up on points.

He opened the second round in good style—quick and free and light—and in the midst of it suddenly I saw him make up his mind for a heavy left. I leant forward, bracing my right leg, covering my jaw with my left hand, and gliding over his coming arm with my right. There was a delicious shock, and Grenfell, lifted clean off his feet, collapsed on the floor.

The *Daily Mail* of 3 March 1909 described this blow as ' rather by accident'. But no more deliberately planned hit was ever delivered.

Thereafter we had an exciting evening at Exeter. Dicky Spread had prepared a grand repast in my rooms in College, and thither proceeded the College squad, all enthusiasm for the victory over Balliol. From that time onwards I became of Exeter College a part, and the place a part of me. I had done something for it.

Yes, we celebrated that night at Exeter. The next evening, moreover, a party of us foregathered in the rooms of Putnam of Christ Church, champion hammer-thrower of the 'Varsity. And we drank largely of ' Five X ', and finally left Tom Quad, giving as pass-word, by Putnam's instruction, the name of ' the biggest bounder at the House '—which I have now forgotten. And as we came to Carfax we heard ourselves singing mightily, and we were just in the midst of arranging to part and fly in different directions should we see any sign of the Proctor, when, curiously enough, we found ourselves taking off our caps to that very man. Dicky Spread was the only one of us to escape the ' Name and College, please ', he having casually donned somebody's gown by way of a muffler.

That was Saturday night—the Prelims. having taken place on Friday. On Sunday I went up to London for the day—without leave of absence. It chanced that I missed the last train to Oxford and was stranded at the Paddington Hotel.

I arrived back in Oxford early on Monday morning and found two notes awaiting me. One was from the Sub-Proctor requesting me to wait on him at one o'clock (that was for being away from College without leave; it might mean gating, or a fine, or being sent down—I did not know which); the other was from Thornewill, the Captain of the Boxing Club, saying that the Blues Committee were not satisfied whether Grenfell or I was the better man to represent Oxford against Cambridge; we would therefore box again on Tuesday—the following afternoon. Here was a tough mouthful to chew as I wandered disconsolately to visit the Proctor! What a miserable morning it was, too ; wet and clammy, dark and draughty. Having been fined by the Proctor—a genial soul delighted to do a small stroke of business for the benefit of the University— I went round to the High to curse Thornewill. What, I asked, was the use of carefully planning a stratagem if idiotic judges confused chance with intention ?

Thornewill replied that he told Grenfell on Saturday, and Grenfell was in hard training for the morrow. I thought of ' Five X ' and cigars, and departed in wrath. I had no conviction this time that I should win. For all

I could tell Grenfell would get his Blue, and the work for which I was striving would be crippled or delayed. The next afternoon, without a friend to bear me company, I stalked grimly down to the Gymnasium. Grenfell and the judges were already there.

'This is rot,' whispered Grenfell.

'Yes,' I agreed.

We stripped and entered the ring. We were both nervous and fought restrainedly and overcarefully. Then in the middle of the second round Grenfell caught me a terrific welt on the nose. The ring swam before me, I felt my knees weaken in a curious way. In an instant Grenfell sprang in to follow up. I saw his chin in the air, his right hand drawn back for a *coup de grâce*. I bent a little to evade his lead and hooked him my outstretched left. Such a little blow it was! Just four inches; but it was the right thing in the right place. Grenfell staggered back and in another moment was against the ropes. Try as I would I could not knock him out; but at the end of the third round, when Time was called, I knew from experience and from Grenfell's face who would get the Blue. He and I stepped stiffly out of the ring, and began putting on our overcoats before going downstairs to the bath-room. We were chatting on generalities when Thornewill came up to me, led me a little to one side, and asked me in a low tone if I would represent the 'Varsity against Cambridge.

'Very pleased,' I said. And I saw Grenfell's face, and shook his hand, and said that I was sorry we could not both represent Oxford. He asked me to have tea with him and his mother that afternoon, but I refused because I had some people coming to tea with me.

I have often regretted that refusal; I should have liked to meet Grenfell's mother.

A few days later we boxing men went down to Cambridge, and I suffered defeat at the hands of Mr. Portway, the Cambridge captain. But I had no reason to be ashamed of the defeat, for he won on points, and I was but little behind; moreover, he was a man of reputation and beat the Oxford representative four years in succession—a record, I think. But Oxford won that year in Boxing and Fencing, 6–2.

So the next day, with a nose out of joint, a broken tooth, and plenty of other wounds—not least, at the time, that I had failed to win my bout—I returned to Oxford and sat for a chemistry exam. in the afternoon, and a few days later the 'Varsity went down, and I went to East Grinstead.

The Oxford life, to any one who truly lives it, leaves no room for regrets. I found myself completely absorbed by the spirit of the place. I trained vigorously; as long as there was a game to play I played it. I was a member of several wine-clubs, debating societies, and nondescript but pleasing associations like the 'Paralytics'. I entertained a little, and was entertained a great deal. I shirked but few card-parties, though I neglected roulette and the turf. Before I left Oxford I was on speaking and dining acquaintance with perhaps as many men as any man at the University.

I was a member of the Remnants Club at the time of their famous dinner at the New Masonic; I was lance-corporal in King Edward's Horse, thus doing what I could towards serving my King, and I was asked to qualify for the position of lieutenant in that body, though

for this I could not make time—greatly to my regret. I
ran with the Exeter beagles and the Exeter boat, played
for my College at rugger and tennis, and boxed for the
University. I found time to watch an occasional 'Varsity
match, and to cheer at a College soccer or hockey event.

Never did spring pass but I was out in the green fields
up Woodstock or Banbury Road, or over Boar's Hill, or
Cumnor, or Shotover, drinking in the song of the larks,
and revelling in the freshness of the first daisies and
yellow aconite.

But in my packed Oxford life my chances of walks
were all too few. I had much correspondence to keep up
—in my second and third years my correspondence was
at times enormous, and made day and night miserable.
I made friends here, there, and everywhere. I did a considerable amount of work too—I simply *had* to, in order
to pass exams., being one of those unfortunate people
who cannot learn without labour. And to make the
labour more difficult I was handicapped with poor health.
My old friend malaria, whom I had bearded in a hundred
stricken swamps, was ever on the look-out for times of
weakness. When I was overworked—as often happened
—he laid his hot hands upon me, goading me into fevers
that burned from my tired senses the best that was in
them, leaving me dog-weary. When I caught a chill
Chindebvu Mangiri sent icy shivers along my spine, and
hot flashes through my eyes, and made my speech jumbled
and over-eager and uncontrollable.

And hundreds of men lived as full a life as I, excepting
always that they were not scheming for the emigration
of homeless children, for that was *my* work and not another's. They cost something, those crowded hours, and

the purpose and passionate resolve. I shall not forget the nights of exhaustion and bitter weariness, when I lay awake going over the present, scheming out the future again and again, hoping and doubting with a mind that was so tired that it would no longer rest.

But not for the gold of Ophir would I exchange one hour of that Oxford life. A score of faces flit through my memory and bring back the glory of those days; and for all time I give thanks to Allah and to Cecil Rhodes.

XXIII

AN END AND A BEGINNING

Is this a holy thing to see
In a rich and fruitful land,
Babes reduced to misery,
Fed with cold and usurous hand? . . .

And their sun does never shine,
And their fields are bleak and bare,
And their ways are fill'd with thorns;
It is eternal winter there.

WILLIAM BLAKE (*Songs of Experience*).

I BEGAN to write on Child Emigration—it seemed to me the best way to make the matter known. In parenthesis let me explain here that when I use the word ‘ I ’ in connexion with the scheme I mean ‘ we ’; for she who is now my wife went every step of the way with me, when she was not travelling a steeper way than mine.

It was Frank Day who solved the problem for me.

‘ Speak,’ he said, ‘ don’t write.’

He was enthusiastic about it, seeing the advantage, as an emigrant, of the child over the man; and he had hopes that Canada would take the matter up.

My friend Alec Johnston was interested, too. Both Day and Johnston were pillars of strength to me in those days.

Things were looking very bright when I received a set-back in the form of a letter from the British South Africa Company, saying that they considered Rhodesia

too young a country in which to start Child Emigration ;
they could not therefore entertain any idea of furthering
the scheme. I had always imagined the first Farm School
on the Rhodesian high-veld, the country which I knew
and loved. Since, however, they would not give me the
land—which was all I asked for—I determined to leave
Rhodesia alone for the present and to apply to the High
Commissioner for Canada, and to the Agents-General
for the Australian and other states.

The following August I went with my regiment to
Salisbury Plain. What a grand time we had on the old
Plain ! There, in a small tent, was held the first meeting
—informal, I admit—on the subject of Child Emigration.
It was my friend Rudall's doing. He suggested that I
should, the following term, give an address on Child
Emigration at the Colonial Club. He got together in
his tent McDonnell, the President of the Club, and
seven or eight other men, and we held our meeting.
In the end McDonnell promised to give me the first
speech-night of the coming term—i. e. 19 October, 1909,
and every man present promised not only to come but
to be a foundation member of a society for actually setting the work afoot.

I went back to East Grinstead rejoicing, to meet my
old friend James Morrell. I was next day to see Sir
Edward Morris, Premier of Newfoundland, and was
exercised in my mind as to how much land I should ask
him for. I consulted James.

‘ Shall I say five thousand acres ? ’

‘ Fifty thousand,’ said James, ‘ always ask for ten times
more than you want.’

So when I saw the Premier of Newfoundland I asked

him for fifty thousand acres with a river or sea-board frontage.

'Very good,' said Sir Edward, 'you shall have it—the best of the land that is open for settlement. And, see here, we'll pay you a bonus on every acre of land you clear, and we'll give you a grant that will cover the salary of a couple of teachers.'

Fate has willed it that the first farm-school has been started in Western Australia. But if God pleases we shall one day take up Sir Edward's offer. My heart has always turned towards that dim island and ancient colony.

With Sir Edward's promise to lift my courage high, I set to work to prepare my speech for the Colonial Club. The thought of it sometimes terrified me; I remember sitting whole days in my little room in an agony of apprehension. How should I make them see?

I was not afraid of the ordeal of facing a crowd. But I was afraid that my speech would not sound right: that it might leave the Club uninterested: that it might serve only as a check to Child Emigration.

Day was gone to Canada, but A. G. Cameron and I had long talks about the scheme.

Time passed swiftly, and it seemed but a moment before the night of the speech arrived. Cameron and I, both very silent, dined together and walked round to the Japanese Café in the High, where the Club's meetings were held.

I expected an audience of about twenty, for this number constituted a fairly good turn out of Rhodes Scholars and other Colonials at the 'Varsity—for the Colonials on the whole have no clique, but blend with the Public

School men and other units of their own Colleges. But this evening they turned up in force. Fifty men were present before the President called order. The benches and chairs were all filled. In there amongst the smoke and chatter were men from every part of the Empire— opposite to me was a Count from the Channel Isles, on my left a little man with a powerful, thoughtful face—a Canadian professor. I saw the iron jaw of Cameron of Prince Edward Island; the thin dark face of a Queenslander; the ingenuous gaze of a South African Rugby Blue; the bull-necked sturdiness of New Zealand; the wide open, untroubled eyes of a Newfoundlander. These fifty men were animated by no common shibboleth, no predetermined party feeling, no single interest that would tend to make them all think alike. Each man thought and hoped separately. My appeal would indeed have to be a deep one and a wide if it were to stir all these various hearts. I was to plead my case before an Imperial Parliament where every member was wholly an Independent.

Suddenly there fell a brief silence, and I heard my name spoken.

I was on my feet, telling them of the thing that had brought me to Oxford. It was not a simple thing to explain, and it was still more difficult to endow it with life.

I told them I believed that imperial unity was not a phrase or an artificial thing. Great Britain and Greater Britain are and must be one. Each is in a position to confer untold benefits upon the other; interdependence is therefore their only possible relation.

The colonies have, above all things, a superfluity of

land for the landless men of Britain; Britain has a superfluity of men for the manless land. But whereas the land
is good land, the men Britain can spare best are not
always good men. The best emigrant farmers have been
the aristocracy of English yeomen, such as England can
ill afford to lose. The colonies should take something
that England does not need, if both sides are to profit;
something nevertheless that will be an asset to the
colony.

Now there are in England over sixty thousand ' de-
pendent ' children—children, orphans or homeless, who
are being brought up in institutions, who will be put
into small jobs at the age of twelve or fourteen, jobs
for which they become too old at eighteen. They have
no parents, and no one standing in any such relation to
them. What have they before them that can be called
a future ?

Here and now, I said, let us found a society to take
as many as we can of these children overseas, to train
them in our own colonies for colonial farm-life. We
want ' schools of agriculture ' in every part of the Empire
where good land is lying empty for lack of men. This
will not be charity, it will be an imperial investment.
There will be no pauper stain attaching to our farm-
schools; every child will be worth far more than the
price of his training to the colony he will eventually help
to build.

Our chief care, I said, must be to entrust the training
of these children only to men and women truly and fully
able to undertake it; there is no such wasteful economy
as cheap schoolmastering. There must be no such
mistake over our farm-schools. Farming is in itself a

wonderful educator; moreover, there is a homeliness about farm-life which makes it the antithesis of existence in an institution. I told them that the Premier of Newfoundland had already promised us fifty thousand acres of good land. Finally, I asked them to join in a work which should be for the good of England and the Empire.

I sat down amid what seemed a very intense silence. Throughout the whole speech no one had made a sound. No chair was shuffled, no one coughed. The only sound that came to me was the dull echo of footsteps, motor-horns, and voices out in the High. I was a little perplexed. Then it gradually dawned upon me that the speech had been successful. I looked round at the men's faces, and saw their eyes fixed upon me. The President, a Canadian, was leaning forward with his elbows on the table.

Half a dozen men rose to ask questions. They were pertinent questions touching heredity, legality, finance; they were put bluntly and searchingly, as if the questioners wished to know. I answered each in turn, easily and fluently, for my heart was uplifted. The hope of twelve years was burning in my brain. I saw the farm-schools as they would be—as they had been a thousand times in my dreams. In the seasons of boisterous health, in the long times when I tossed in the wasting grip of malaria, I had pictured the farm-schools of to-morrow. Now was come the eve of to-morrow. To-morrow I should see them with my living eyes. The past lay in my left hand, the future in my right; I was too fully armed to heed the present.

Yet the present was slowly forcing itself upon me.

I heard Cameron proposing, and Dr. Waddy seconding, that we fifty men should declare ourselves the Society for the Furtherance of Child Emigration to the Colonies. I was instructed to ' carry on ', to collect money, to find the way. We each undertook to pay five shillings to the ' Fund '. A paper was passed round the room; we signed, and the paper was given to me.

At a late hour we disbanded, and I wandered back to Exeter College hardly knowing where I was. According to the custom, I kicked on the old gate that is braced and riveted with iron, and Hookham (entering my name for a ' late ' fine) let me in. I wandered into the main quad, feeling strangely lost, and then on to my staircase and my room.

' The Way,' I thought, ' that is it. I am still to find the Way. But we are on it. We—that's it—fifty of us now . . . My Child Emigration thought is spoken—it is become part of the world.'

My little dingy room, with its photographs and scattered books—how it seemed to have changed! I wandered idly about the room. I became aware that I was dog-tired; my legs ached. One gives of one's best; and it is gone. One has come a little nearer to the dust, whither we all go. Virtue had passed out from me; how little might remain I did not know.

I thought a good sleep would restore me. I heard myself saying, ' Now I will go to sleep '. Then I counted up to an incredible number. I counted innumerable sheep; I made my mind a complete blank—all to no good. So I set about revolving in my mind scheme after scheme—all bearing upon the theme: how to find the way, how to find the money.

With every new hour pealed the bells. One would begin, a little prematurely, perhaps, for Oxford time is not strictly accurate; then another bell would join in; then two or three bells together; then a whole crash of them, gradually ceasing and dying down to silence. Before I left Oxford I came to know the sound of every bell.

It is very quiet at night between the hours of one and five. And in those quiet hours before the dawn come thronging back all the wise things one might have said and all the great things one might have done. Griefs that daylight never knows knock against one's heart, and it needs more than a little valour to meet them. Faults of one's childhood come back too—small deceptions, mistakes that covered one with an agony of shame. One wonders if they are quite forgotten. Just before dawn is the hour of regret. It is said that many people die just before dawn; it would be kinder if they could die sooner.

Lying awake, so, I came to have dreams of the Empire made perfect—through her sons. Many of us dream so at night; then with day it seems that a reaction sets in, a kind of madness seizes the whole world, and hate and jealousy and vanity set us all shouting and squabbling again.

During that October night—the night of the founding of the Child Emigration Society—all these things crowded into my head. Through the bells came at times the surge of the hill wind sweeping through Chitaka's kraal, or the sound of big game crushing the dead leaves of the low-veld. Sometimes I saw my father standing on the hot road near Christmas Pass; sometimes I saw

A a

him stooping over my cot to sing to me. But always my mind came back to the problem before me—how to find the way and the money.

After a long while the grey dawn-light stole gradually round the buttresses of the overshadowing chapel, and in through the dusty diamond panes. The day was come. How often have I lain awake to watch it! For the gods are not always kind to the seekers of new ways.

EPILOGUE

BY

SIR ARTHUR LAWLEY, K.C.M.G., G.C.S.I.

THE story which Kingsley Fairbridge has had to tell in the preceding pages is one of conflict with the forces of nature from the very beginning to the end of his all too short life. Before his childhood days were over he was brought face to face with danger and difficulty, and emerged from each ordeal with fresh courage and nobility of soul. He was a Rhodes Scholar whose early years were spent in regions remote from civilization, an undergraduate cherishing a purpose which one day or another should contribute to the solution of a great Imperial Problem, and that is : how to combine the work of Child Rescue with that of Emigration. He emerged to manhood an idealist who combined his idealism with marvellous fertility of resource.

Every year tens of thousands of boys and girls seek admission to the labour market only to be told that there is no need of them, and they are flung back on to one or other of the great human scrap-heaps which lie at the gates of every one of our great cities—derelict little vessels on the Ocean of Life, children doomed to a blind alley existence and the squalor of the slums. His plan was simple enough. It was to take some at least of these little people before they were contaminated by their evil surroundings and to carry them off to a land of sunshine, there to be trained to become strong, sturdy, and efficient citizens able to play their part in developing the vast resources of Australia—a land where the prizes of life are open to all. He has told us how that scheme became all-absorbing—something to live for, to work for, and, as he showed, to die for. It is unfortunate that his autobiography should come to an end just at the moment when his life-dream became inspired with life and took concrete shape.

From the start Kingsley Fairbridge shouldered the burden and faced the difficulties by which the launching of his pet project was beset. It would have been well if he could have told us how those difficulties (and they were many) were overcome. As it is, we can only endeavour to sketch in outline the development of the Scheme which came into existence in the Colonial Club in Oxford that chill October evening of 1909.

During the year 1910 a small but influential Committee was formed to carry into effect the aims of the Child Emigration Society. Major Slessor and Mrs. Cuthbert Baynes became Chairman and Secretary, while Mrs. Haldane, Mrs. Phillips, and Sir James Douie as members of the Committee did yeoman service. Among Fairbridge's undergraduate friends A. E. K. Slingsby, A. L. Johnston, and J. C. Stollery were enthusiastic helpers—all of them afterwards being killed in the Great War. By the end of the year they had collected some £2,000. This sum seems hardly adequate to the launching of so ambitious an enterprise, but nevertheless it was resolved that a start should be made. One can only wonder at the confidence and courage which Fairbridge was called on to display at this and at every stage of his life's work, and which never failed him. Fortunately, he had by his side from earliest undergraduate days a comrade worthy to share his ideals, and hand in hand with him to face the priva-

tions and hardships of a Pioneer Existence. The fact
that neither of them was richly endowed with this world's
goods did not daunt them. It did not seem to occur to
either of them that because their circumstances were
straitened their wedding should be postponed, and in
December 1911 they were married.

Simultaneously their passages were booked on board a
crowded emigrant ship sailing in March 1912, which
reached Albany after five weeks of inevitable discomfort,
seeing that their fellow-passengers were for the most
part rough emigrants and that the crowd on board was
great. After a week in Albany they pushed on to Perth,
where they made many good friends who, from the first,
have maintained their interest in the Fairbridge Farm
School, as it came to be called. Meanwhile messages
from England were frequent and insistent, urging im-
mediate preparation for the arrival of the first batch of
children, as it was found impossible to go on collecting
subscriptions unless a start could be made. There was
no time to lose. Fairbridge and his wife were strangers
in this vast territory of Western Australia—a land of
magnificent distances—ignorant of its conditions, new
to its ways. The cash at their disposal was but scanty.
Transport was often difficult to secure. It was, however,
absolutely necessary to find some suitable cottage capable
of accommodating the party and to find it at once. A
small farm of 160 acres was found not far from Pinjarra
which had been the Receiving Home for lads from a
Ragged Home in Liverpool, and this was purchased in
spite of its deficiencies and disadvantages on the principle
of ' Any port in a storm '.

Time pressed. Much had to be done to get this four-roomed shanty fit for occupation before the boys arrived from England. The purchase of the property included a certain amount of livestock and an orchard where pruning had been sadly neglected. A gardener and his wife should have been there to run the house and farm; but their arrival was delayed and the only help forthcoming was temporary at the hands of two or three young men who looked in to lend a hand for a time. While everything was in disorder Fairbridge went down with a very sharp attack of malaria, from which he recovered to welcome the arrival of a little daughter on the scene. Thanks to the skill of the doctor and the kindly ministrations of the proprietress of the hotel at Pinjarra all went well with mother and child, and soon Fairbridge himself threw off all traces of malaria. The orchard was pruned, a vegetable garden was laid out. A young Irishman came in to lend a hand and stayed for six months, rendering invaluable aid. As summer advanced the heat grew more intense, but nevertheless preparations had to be made to house the children whose advent was imminent. By January it had been found possible to run up some temporary shelters, half a dozen cotton tents and a hessian roof which formed the dining-room. When these preparations were completed Fairbridge went down to Fremantle to meet the first little party of orphans.

These early days were never free from anxiety and worry. The new-comers rejected country fare such as fresh vegetables and fruit: they could not drink milk and they clamoured for meat and potatoes, which latter were not at first available. Another great trouble arose in that the Government refused to help in the matter of education. This meant that those 12 little boys aged from seven to twelve years had to be found some employment to fill in the long summer days. The elder boys soon learnt the simpler farm operations, also to help with the kitchen and laundry work. But it is not easy to get small children to do monotonous work with any regularity. The hard daily grind of keeping these little chaps to their work, encouraging them, infusing everything with cheerfulness and interest, all fell on Fairbridge's shoulders. It was of no use to tell the children to play when work was finished. They did not know how to play, and quarrelling was rife, but soon a new tone became evident, and a complete change in the bearing and the manners of all the boys. Throughout the summer Fairbridge was constantly down with malaria, and during an attack the boys would often carry his bed down to the orchard, and there he would lie in the shade of a great apricot tree reading to the boys and explaining what he read, oblivious of the fever which racked his limbs. With the end of summer came the completion of a new building into which a move was made, and the comfort of the inmates was vastly increased.

In June 1913 the second party of 22 boys was due to arrive. In anticipation of their coming Fairbridge was luckily able to employ a builder to put up two sleeping sheds, open to the air, as dormitories for the party, while he himself, although not versed in carpentry, made from the roughest of material beds for the 22 boys as well as tables and forms for the dining-room. In a word he practically furnished the Home. Moreover, with help from Mr. Austin, he painted and oiled all buildings inside and out, distempered the walls, and painted the roofs.

Great difficulties were experienced in providing educa-

tion for 30 odd children, but eventually these difficulties were overcome and the new boys settled down
quickly and happily. All was going well when the out-
break of war threatened the undertaking with total collapse. The scheme had only been carried to its present
state by constant labour and strenuous endeavour. At
times the struggle had seemed desperate and the undertaking impossible of achievement. Remote though it
was, war brought in its train conditions which formed a
deadly menace to all that had been achieved hitherto.
Of the few male members of the Staff, which never
numbered more than two at any one time, all who could
pass the medical test went away to the War. Ultimately
three of them—Allen, Hartfield, and Alec Bond—gave
up their lives for their country. Fairbridge's malaria was
responsible for his rejection, and he remained to run the
Farm School. But for him the School must inevitably
have broken up, and the experiment would have been
written down a failure.

The members of the Oxford Committee were dispersed
on war work of various descriptions and had little time
to devote to Child Emigration. Subscriptions fell off,
and early in the year the Oxford Committee telegraphed
instructions to Fairbridge to close down. He, however,
backed by the Perth Committee, undertook to carry on
if £400 could be sent from England. A promise to that
effect was forthcoming, and thanks for the devoted labour
of Miss Dorothy Lane Poole, who during the whole four
years of the War carried on the work almost single handed,
the Committee were able to keep their promise, and so
the work went on; but if the struggle had been serious
before it now became almost desperate. Fortunately at

this juncture Providence sent Miss Dennehy to undertake the secretarial work. Her help was then, and is now, simply invaluable. At one time closure seemed inevitable, but Fairbridge was able to make a bargain with the State Authorities that, if they would make a weekly grant of 4*s* per head, he would keep the School going. So the struggle went on. Economy in every department was the order of the day ; repairs were not done; renewals were not made; and debts were increasing.

During these difficult times Fairbridge had the offer of more than one attractive, well-paid billet, but his devotion to his ideal and his loyalty to the School led him to resist each one however advantageous it might appear. It was by his self-surrender and sacrifice that the Farm School was enabled to survive those perilous days; but Peace came at last, and with it fresh resolve and determination in the mind of the Founder to carry his scheme to a successful issue. He was greatly encouraged in this direction by the fact that of the 34 lads brought out before 1914 every one had made good and was qualified to go on to the land familiar with the rudiments of farming and the conditions of life in Australia. Still more was he encouraged by the staunch and loyal helpmeet who, through all the seven years and more of stress and strain of the Old Farm bore, as only a brave and unselfish woman can, the whole brunt of domestic administration, often single-handed but ever with courage undaunted and never-failing care for others, braving the hardships of a Pioneer. There are but few who realize how greatly Mrs. Fairbridge contributed by her personal influence and tact to the successful launching of this remarkable enterprise !

When the War came to an end, the finances of each European Power were in a deplorable state. The enormous losses in every theatre of war seemed to render hopeless any attempt to raise a substantial sum of money for such a proposition as Fairbridge had in view. Nevertheless, he made his plans to visit England, though before sailing he had much to do. He had, as a preliminary to his arrival at Home, to draw up a programme of meetings in England and Scotland. He had to secure definitely the grant of 5s. per head per week from the State Government of Western Australia for a School of 200 children (boys and girls). He had to make provision for the carrying on of the School in his absence. The coffers were depleted ; the Staff were reduced to one (Dick Fryer Smith) beside Miss Dennehy. The boys were by now sufficiently advanced to go out into the world and command a wage of say 15s. to £1 a week. At the School they could not hope to receive more than 5s. a week. To ask them to remain was to ask them to give up a substantial sum, but every boy volunteered to stay and keep the School going, no matter what the monetary loss to each one might be. On arrival in England Fairbridge received an invitation to speak before the Oversea Settlement Committee, at whose hands he received great encouragement. He spent eight months in England, and by the time that he again set sail for Western Australia he had got together a sum of £27,000. During that time the Central Office of the Child Emigration Society was transferred from Oxford to London.

Experience had shown that there were many disadvantages attaching to the small farm which Fairbridge had bought, and it was resolved to sell it and start afresh on a more suitable site of 3,200 acres which was offered on very reasonable terms. It seemed ideal for the purpose, and at once Fairbridge set to work to build on plans on which he had been at work for no little time. A more difficult time in which to build could not have been found. Prices of material and labour went soaring upwards. No contractor would quote anything like a reasonable figure, and Fairbridge had to become his own buyer and clerk of the works. Delays were incessant, and for the moment it was necessary to keep the old farm going as a half-way house between London and the new Pinjarra. In 1921 boys and girls began to arrive from England and had to be housed in the old farm, and only moved into the new farm as cottage by cottage was built and furnished. For a time Fairbridge and some of his staff were in a temporary camp. Twice at this time he had to go across to Melbourne in an endeavour to obtain a grant from the Commonwealth Government similar to that provided by the State Government. In June 1922 he got word that his request was granted, and with this in his pocket he hurried back to England hoping to secure a similar grant from the British Government. It was during this journey that his illness first began to manifest itself. His sufferings were acute; but in spite of intense physical pain he got through an immense amount of work, and his mission was entirely successful. He returned to Pinjarra in January 1923, and at long last he found himself comfortably bestowed in a well-built house of his own with his wife and four children, after years of discomfort and homelessness. Despite his sufferings, which increased day by day, Fairbridge kept steadily before him the ideal which was the mainspring of his life.

During his last years he saw the strengthening of the Society by the active and liberal co-operation of Dr. Barnardo's, from whom we got 100 children in February 1924, doubling our numbers in a single night. Their advent necessitated the carrying out of a liberal building programme which provided ample accommodation for 200 children as well as that of the Staff. To-day there are 207 children at the school; there are forty substantial buildings which have been put up and furnished at a cost of over £23,000; in addition over £10,000 has been expended on the development of the land. Of this total sum at least £30,000 has been found by the Child Emigration Society in Great Britain. It is a remarkable achievement that within a few years, and before Kingsley Fairbridge went far away into the Silent Land, he should see the fulfilment of his heart's desire and a Farm School firmly established in which the policy should be the development of Character, Health, and Ability.

These are the three main planks of our platform! We want to bring up the children as capable clean-minded Christian men and women and good Australian citizens. To help us in this task we have a strong local Committee in Western Australia, including several of the leading citizens of Perth, whose assistance to and active co-operation with the London Committee have been simply invaluable. At home we have the sympathy and generous support of the Oversea Settlement Department of the Dominions Office. The London Committee have but one resolve and that is to uphold through dark days and fair the ideals of their Founder, Kingsley Fairbridge.